the book of
the covenant

The Bible's unfolding story of
relationship with God

B N Howard

D0862112

thegoodbook
COMPANY

The book of the covenant
The Bible's unfolding story of relationship with God

© B N Howard 2013

Published by
The Good Book Company
Tel (UK): 0333–123–0880;
International: +44 (0) 208 942 0880
Email: admin@thegoodbook.co.uk

Websites:
UK: www.thegoodbook.co.uk
North America: www.thegoodbook.com
Australia: www.thegoodbook.com.au
New Zealand: www.thegoodbook.co.nz

ISBN: 9781908317735

Cover design: Steve Devane
Illustrations: André Parker
Author photo: Rachel Friedlander
Printed and bound by CPI Group (UK) Ltd, Croydon, CR0 4YY

Contents

To Jonathan Fletcher

How beautiful on the mountains
are the feet of those who bring good news
Isaiah 52 v 7

Preface

There has been a rediscovery in recent years of Biblical theology. It's an approach to the Bible that seeks to understand any individual part of Scripture in the context of the whole. It asks the question: *What is the "Big Story" of the Bible, of which this is just a part?* It's an important question that has opened up new ways of thinking about the gospel message, new ways of preaching, and a new attitude to the Old Testament that has rescued believers from using it unhelpful ways – as though it were merely a story book of morality tales.

Out of this, there has come an exciting proliferation of books and study courses that call themselves "Bible overviews". The average reader could be forgiven for being a little confused by the differences between them, until we realise that there are many different kinds of overview. Because the Bible is a rich and complex story, there are many different routes through that are legitimate ways of revealing the magnificence of God's loving purposes in the world.

Some are *historical* – they trace the timeline of God's saving acts chronologically, because the order of the books of the Bible as we have them are not arranged in time order.

Others are *thematic*, based on a variety of theological strands that run through the Bible – of the King and his Kingdom, or of God's promise to make for himself a blessed people in a blessed land, or of the promise of a saviour and the fulfilment in Christ, or of the gathering and scattering of God's people. It's important to recognise that these are not *competing* views of Scripture. They are simply different ways to read the Bible that yield their own unique insights, and combine to give us a fuller view of the wisdom and glory of our great God.

This very readable volume is a further addition to this helpful body of literature. It is an overview that focuses on *covenants* in the Bible – the "deals" that God made with his people which all find their fulfilment in the new covenant made through Jesus' death on the cross.

This is an important and foundational strand to understand, because these covenants are the basis on which the faith of Old Testament believers rested, and to which they constantly referred in their worship and in their daily lives.

The author (Bernard to some, Nick to others), has done a brilliant job of presenting and applying here much of the seminal work of O. Palmer Robertson, whose book *The Christ of the Covenants* remains a key text for many theological students, but is indigestible to most at over 300 pages!

For clarity's sake, you need to know that this is *not* a book that rests upon, or is about what is sometimes called "federal vision", a different theological approach entirely.

But it *is* a book that takes the Bible seriously, and not only informs us about how the various covenants of the Bible work together, but also explores the ways that they are still relevant today to those of us who are beneficiaries of *the eternal covenant* through faith in Christ.

My prayer is that you enjoy and benefit from reading this book as much as I have from helping to bring it into being.

Tim Thornborough
Editor, February 2013

Introduction

I was standing on the edge of the English village of Burmarsh, looking out over Romney Marsh. After bad experiences getting lost in the past, this time I'd brought a detailed map with me, showing every single house and footpath. After finding my position and working out where I was going, I started folding up the map so I could tuck it away again.

Fifteen minutes later, already exhausted without having taken a step, I'd produced a messy bundle of paper that hardly resembled the original compact rectangle. I knew I needed to use the map's built-in creases, but I couldn't figure out how to do that correctly.

Just as maps help us find our way in unknown terrain, so the Bible guides us through the hopes, trials, disappointments and joys of life. It's easy to take wrong turns in this world. Proverbs 19 v 2 warns us:

> It is not good to have zeal without knowledge,
>> nor to be hasty and miss the way.

The Bible gives us the knowledge we need to choose the best paths. It speaks to us of God and his glory, tells us how to receive his salvation, and teaches us how to please him in all things.

The trouble is, reading the Bible can be very similar to using a large map. It's such a big book that we can struggle to handle it properly. It's not hard to end up with an untidy bundle of misunderstandings. In the Bible's case, the "creases" that make all the difference are the seven covenants between God and mankind. **Part One** of this book will explain what a covenant is, and show how the Bible's seven covenants fit together to be one united covenant (which is why the Bible is "the Book of the Covenant"). **Part Two** will look into the meaning of each of the seven divine covenants. And **Part Three** will explain how to use these "creases" when reading the Bible.

Today, in the west at least, we have free and easy access to the Bible. There are multiple copies on our shelves. But in practice there are huge chunks of Scripture that might as well not be there, because we never read them. We encounter the Bible through sermons in church, home-group studies, and the portions measured out to us in daily reading notes. As a result we're not complete strangers to the Bible, but we don't know the whole book anything like as well as we should. Getting familiar with the covenants can change that. They show how the entire Bible fits together, so we can engage more comfortably with all its different parts. The aim of this Bible overview is to help our generation truly become "people of the Book", to the glory of God.

Part One

God's Offer of Covenant Relationship

Chapter 1

What Is a Covenant?

Many Christians would agree that covenants are very important without being able to put their finger on what exactly a covenant is.

It's right to note their importance. Take some of the Bible topics most likely to be taught in children's groups at church: Noah's ark, "Father Abraham", the Ten Commandments, King David, and the Last Supper. In each case a covenant is central.[1] As a recent book puts it: "Covenant spreads its wings throughout the Bible. It is a theme we cannot ignore if we desire to know the God of the Scriptures, because he reveals himself as a 'covenant making and covenant keeping God.'"[2] The IVP *New Bible Dictionary* says that the covenant theme is "the most important link between the Testaments."[3] And J.I. Packer points out: "The whole Bible is, as it were, presented by Jesus Christ to the church and to each Christian as the book of the covenant."[4]

So it crops up often and is obviously hugely significant, but what does this word "covenant" actually mean? To put it as simply as possible, *a covenant is a deal*. But covenants are especially meaningful and serious deals, as we can tell from looking at some of the relevant Bible passages.

Let's start with a minor covenant in the book of Genesis – not one of the covenants between God and mankind, but a covenant agreed between Isaac and Abimelech, a Philistine king:

Genesis 26 v 26-29

Meanwhile, Abimelech had come to [Isaac] from Gerar, with Ahuzzath his personal adviser and Phicol the commander of his forces. Isaac asked them, "Why have you come to me, since you were hostile to me and sent me away?"

They answered, "We saw clearly that the LORD was with you; so we said, 'There ought to be a sworn agreement between us' – between us and you. Let us make a treaty [literally: cut a covenant] with you that you will do us no harm, just as we did not molest you but always treated you well and sent you away in peace."

The final sentence shows that covenants are deals that create lasting relationships. Abimelech wants to be on good terms with Isaac, so he suggests they make a covenant to bring about that new relationship.

For a covenant to be successful, words need to be involved. Lasting relationships are not created by a wink and a smile. The covenant between Isaac and Abimelech must have included spoken terms because Abimelech says he wants a "sworn agreement". Spoken terms of agreement are so essential to covenants that in Psalm 105 the psalm-writer uses "word" as an alternative way of saying "covenant": "He remembers his *covenant* for ever, the *word* he commanded, for a thousand generations" (Psalm 105 v 8).

Perhaps what we've seen so far brings marriage to mind – two people entering into a new relationship by making an agreement with spoken vows. It's right to think of marriage as an example of a covenant because the Bible itself describes it as a covenant (Malachi 2 v 14).

But we haven't quite got to the bottom of covenants yet. The Bible speaks of people "cutting" a covenant, and there's a reason for that violent-sounding expression. When a covenant was agreed in Old Testament times, there was usually a ceremony with some fairly gruesome cutting.

In Jeremiah chapter 34, for instance, when King Zedekiah and the people of Jerusalem make a covenant with the LORD (verse 15), they cut a calf in two, place the pieces either side of a pathway, and then walk between them. We find out the reason for the blood and guts later on, when God rebukes Zedekiah and the others for failing to keep the covenant they've only just made:

Jeremiah 34 v 18, 20, NKJV

I will give the men who have transgressed My covenant, who have not performed the words of the covenant which they made before Me, when they cut the calf in two and passed between the parts of it ... I will give them into the hand of their enemies and into the hand of those who seek their life. Their dead bodies shall be for meat for the birds of the heaven and the beasts of the earth.

By walking through the pieces of the carcass, the people had effectively said to God: "May we become like this dead calf if we don't keep the covenant we're making today." God's terrifying decree, after they've broken the covenant, holds them to their word. He's saying: "It will be as you said it should be when you walked between those torn animal pieces. You will end up like that calf."

So the blood-soaked opening ceremony is a way of announcing the punishment for covenant failure. By agreeing to this punishment, it's as if the participants are lifting a sword above their own heads. "If we fail to keep the terms of this covenant," they're saying, "may the sword suspended today fall down upon our own necks."

In his book *The Christ of the Covenants*, O. Palmer

Robertson puts it like this: "The parties of the covenant are committed to one another by a ... process of blood-shedding. This blood-shedding represents the intensity of the commitment of the covenant."[5]

Covenants in the Bible are made between people, and also between God and humanity.[6] It's worth pointing out a major difference between those two kinds of covenant. When Isaac and Abimelech make a covenant, they operate as equal partners, which means they both have a say on the terms and conditions. But a glance at any of the divine covenants makes it clear that God alone decides the terms of the covenant. There's no opportunity for the people involved to negotiate a better deal. Their choice is simply to take it or leave it. There's no other way to enter into relationship with God.[7]

It's time to sum up...

A covenant is an agreement establishing a relationship, with life or death consequences. That definition captures the three distinctive elements of a covenant: agreed terms, the resulting relationship, and the fatal consequences of falling short. To compress the definition further, we could say it's **a relationship-creating deal with teeth.**[8]

- **God's willingness to make covenants with mankind shows that he wants to be in relationship with us.** *That's extraordinary.* We have every reason to feel very small and very sinful before God. He's the omnipotent Lord of hosts: thousands upon thousands of powerful angels wait on his command (Matthew 26 v 53). To him, our nations – with their flags, governments, armies and economies – are like a drop of water at the bottom of a bucket (Isaiah 40 v 15). What's more, God's character is unchangingly pure and unfailingly good, while we're so often lazy, selfish, thoughtless and unkind. Time after time we act in a way that grieves God, and that we ourselves know is wrong. And yet God is willing to cut covenants with people like us, proving that he wants to be in relationship with us. We shouldn't respond to this truth by thinking more highly of ourselves, as if we deserve to have covenant dealings with God. No, as Paul reminds new covenant believers: "While we were still sinners, Christ died for us" (Romans 5 v 8). The right way to respond to this truth is with deep wonder, as we meditate on God's willingness to stoop down and make covenants with the likes of us.

- **God's covenant-making teaches us that there's only one way to enter into relationship with him.** We need to reject the "one mountain, many paths" view of God, as if he were sitting at the top of a spiritual mountain with many very different religious paths leading up to his throne at the summit. It's God who determines how people should relate to him. As we've seen, he's the one who sets the terms of the covenant – it's not as if he and mankind negotiate around a boardroom table. When people practise a religion other than Christianity, it's as if they're trying to persuade God to accept their own alternative agreement. They haven't understood that God is the one who decides the terms and conditions, which have been fully and finally revealed in the Bible – the book of the covenant.

- For a similar reason, **we need to keep a close watch over the message we proclaim.** We've seen that covenants are built around carefully chosen words. The good news about Jesus is a covenant – the new covenant – and like other covenants it contains specific terms of agreement. We must therefore take great care to put the correct message across when we're reaching out to non-Christians. If we get the terms and conditions wrong, we'll misinform people on how to be in relationship with God.

- Finally, **the grisly "cutting" feature of covenants explains why blood is so frequently found on the pages of Scripture.** The Bible is a blood-spattered book. Some Bible readers may think the constant references to blood are distasteful. But we've seen that covenants are agreements with life or death consequences. If a covenant isn't kept, blood must be spilt. People conscious of their sin will understand that blood needs to be shed as a result of their failure to keep the covenant. It will either be their own blood or – could it be true! – the blood of a substitute in their place. Believers should rejoice in the substitutionary blood found throughout Scripture's pages.

Chapter 2

The Covenants:
United but Different

Imagine a time of open prayer in a church home group. A man quietly says, *"This is a prayer based on Psalm 137."* He then prays the following verses out loud, replacing the words, "Daughter of Babylon", with "Islamist terrorists":

Psalm 137 v 8-9

O Daughter of Babylon, doomed to destruction,
happy is he who repays you
for what you have done to us –
he who seizes your infants
and dashes them against the rocks.

As the prayer comes to an end, no one joins the man in saying "Amen". There's an extremely long and icy pause.

At last someone speaks up: *"I don't think it's right to pray like that. Jesus tells us to love our enemies."* There's a general murmur of agreement from the others.

"But I was just trying to use the Psalms to help me in my prayer life, as Pastor Alan recommended on Sunday," the man replies.

Someone diplomatically tries saying: *"It's just that some psalms are better for that than others."* But the man furrows his brow and says: *"Didn't Pastor Alan say all the psalms are examples of people addressing God in a divinely-inspired way?"*

"Well, yes, he did, and that's true, but ..."

No one knows quite what to say next.

Eventually someone suggests they all have a fresh cup of coffee and some more cake.

The problem is obvious. While we're quick to use some quotations from the Psalms as model expressions of devotion, we instinctively avoid others like the one above. How would we defend ourselves if someone accused us of being inconsistent?

We face a similar problem when reading other parts of the Bible. We recognise the ongoing significance of commands like "You shall not murder" or "You shall not give false testimony against your neighbour" (Exodus 20 v 13, 16). But when we read Leviticus 19 v 19, "Do not wear clothing woven of two kinds of material", we have a hunch it doesn't apply to us any more, and so we carry on wearing the cotton/polyester mix T-shirt we put on that morning. Once again, however, we're left with the impression that despite all we have in common with God's people from former times, there are also major differences. Is there a way to read the Bible without feeling that we're picking and choosing to suit ourselves?

The solution is *a right understanding of the covenants between God and mankind.* There are seven divine covenants, which come at various points along the Bible's timeline. These covenants click together to form one "eternal covenant" (Hebrews 13 v 20).[9] The things that bring them together unite God's people throughout the ages. But the covenants also have differences. These have the effect of dividing salvation history into separate time zones, with different instructions for each zone. That explains why certain past practices and attitudes no longer apply today.

One eternal covenant

On 7th February 2003, demolition work began on the two white towers of the old Wembley Stadium, London's world-famous sporting venue. People had known for some time that a more up-to-date stadium was needed, but many hoped the iconic white towers would be included in the new design. Instead the architect decided to knock them down completely, with a huge steel arch taking their place as the eye-catching feature of the new stadium.

The sad history of the Wembley towers helps us pose a question about the covenants between God and mankind. When one covenant succeeds another, is the previous one fully knocked down, or are certain parts of the earlier covenant preserved in the next? The Bible's answer is clear: past covenants are built into those that follow, not completely demolished. It's as if those beloved white towers had been incorporated into the new Wembley stadium.

When the Bible speaks about past covenants, we're left in no doubt that parts of them are ongoing. Take a look, for example, at **Ezekiel 37 v 24-26**:

My servant David will be king over them, and they will have one shepherd [an allusion to the covenant with David], and they will walk in my ordinances, and keep my statutes, and observe them [an allusion to the covenant with Moses]. And they shall live on the land that I gave to Jacob my servant, in which your fathers lived [an allusion to the covenant with Abraham] ... and I will make a covenant with them [an allusion to the new covenant].[10]

Ezekiel is describing what life will be like for God's people in the future. It's clear that several different covenants will be fulfilled when that time arrives. The passage demonstrates that one covenant is not abandoned when the next one comes along: certain signature features are preserved.[11]

There's another reason why all the covenants together form one everlasting covenant. Each one has the same heartbeat, the same core theme, which is summed up in the phrase: "I will be your God, and you will be my people".

Covenants create relationships, and God's plan throughout his covenant-making has been to set apart a people for relationship with himself. When he makes his covenant with Abraham, he says: "I will establish my covenant ... to be your God and the God of your descendants after you" (Genesis 17 v 7).

Hundreds of years later, Moses says: "You are standing here in order to enter into a covenant with the LORD your God ... to confirm you this day as his people, that he may be your God" (Deuteronomy 29 v 12-13). The covenant with David shares the same intention: "I the LORD will be their God, and my servant David will be prince among them" (Ezekiel 34 v 24; see also 2 Samuel 7 v 24-26). And when Jeremiah looks ahead to the new covenant he says: "'The time is coming,' declares the LORD, 'when I will make a new covenant ... I will be their God, and they will be my people'" (Jeremiah 31 v 31, 33).

In view of this, we could compare the covenants to a series of connected reservoirs providing water for a city. Each reservoir has certain distinctive features such as its location, capacity and shape, but they all serve the same underlying purpose of meeting the city's need for water. The covenants are united in a similar way by one intention: God's desire to have a people of his own. The eternal covenant is God's provision of relationship with himself, provision that spans all of human history.

Seven different covenants

It's essential to stress the unity of the covenants. But to understand Scripture rightly we also need to grasp the significant differences between them. Sometimes these can be stark. For example, on two separate occasions Jacob sets up a pillar at Bethel as an act of worship without being rebuked by God (Genesis 28 v 18-22; 35 v 14-15). Yet this practice is later fiercely condemned. In the time of the covenant with Moses, it's described as something which "the LORD your God hates" (Deuteronomy 16 v 22). Later on in the Bible, the prophet Samuel transfers the kingship from Saul to David (1 Samuel 15 v 28; 16 v 13), thereby activating a completely new ruling family. But in the next covenant period God decrees that only direct descendants of David should be appointed king (2 Samuel 7 v 12-16).

So the experience of belonging to God's people changes according to whichever covenant is in operation at the time. The covenants are like gates separating the different periods of Bible history. When God's people go through a covenant gate into that covenant's "field", they need to live according to the code of practice for that field. It's true that much stays the same from field to field throughout salvation history. The fields form one covenant valley. In particular, God's people-forming purpose runs through the whole valley like a river. But the different covenants do produce real variation from one field to the next. That explains why physical circumcision, for example, was once compulsory for every boy born to the people of God, but is no longer necessary today. We're in a different covenant field in the valley of salvation.

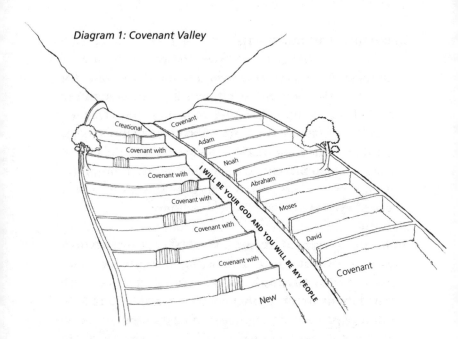

Diagram 1: Covenant Valley

Creational Covenant

Covenant with Adam

Covenant with Noah

Covenant with Abraham

Covenant with Moses

Covenant with David

New Covenant

I WILL BE YOUR GOD AND YOU WILL BE MY PEOPLE

Life lessons

- **Understanding the unity of the covenants, and the differences between them, equips us for reading the Bible.** Why are some passages from the Psalms good for use in prayer today while others are best avoided? Because the covenants are united and yet different. Why should we take some Old Testament commands at face value, and not others? For the same reason. The better we know the covenants, the more mature we'll be in our handling of the Bible.

- **Because of the unity of the covenants, Bible history is *our* family history.** The Bible is like a big family photo album. God's people take part in the same eternal covenant, no matter which salvation period we're in. So the believers we read about in Scripture are our spiritual ancestors, our family members, and that should make their ups and downs more meaningful to us. As we go through similar situations ourselves, we can learn from our family members' experiences in the past. We'll be more likely to avoid their mistakes and take heart from their victories when we see how closely related we are to them, through our shared eternal covenant.

• **The covenantal structure of salvation history shows us that God is a careful planner, who sees things through to the end.** Other gods, like the gods of Greek mythology, never have a long-term strategy in their dealings with mankind. But the God of the Bible has a salvation plan that develops through seven distinct stages, each one contributing to the final outcome. What a magnificent demonstration of long-range planning! It should encourage us to trust God in his personal dealings with us. Perhaps you're at a point in your life where it's hard for you to see how God could possibly meet your needs. The famous words of Psalm 23 verse 1: "The LORD is my shepherd, I shall not be in want", seem to ring hollow for you. But remember that God is a long-term planner. Reflecting on this will refresh your confidence that he will supply what you truly need in his timing.

• *"I will be your God, and you will be my people."* **God is absolutely determined to set apart a people for himself and he won't let anything stop him.** In this way the covenant theme should give God's people great assurance. His insistence on having us as his people means he'll never let us go. And if you're not yet one of his people, don't wait around for something to happen. Jesus says: "All those the Father gives me will come to me" (John 6 v 37). So come. If you don't want to come to him, what are your reasons for hanging back?

- *"I will be your God, and you will be my people."* **Ultimately, belonging to God's covenant people is more about God choosing us than our choosing him.** Paul puts this beyond doubt: "He chose us in him before the creation of the world ... in love" (Ephesians 1 v 4). To be loved before creation is to be loved for a very long time. This is something we need to meditate on until it sinks deeply into our souls. No wonder David says: "Surely goodness and love will follow me all the days of my life" (Psalm 23 v 6) – God's love had already been following him since before the creation of the world. In his love, God not only chooses his people, he calls us (1 Corinthians 1 v 9), cleanses us (1 Corinthians 6 v 11), clothes us (Galatians 3 v 27), commands us (Matthew 28 v 20), chastens us (Hebrews 12 v 6, 10) and carries us (Deuteronomy 33 v 27; Isaiah 46 v 3-4; Jude 24). This is the love that the Christian songwriter Josh Garrels has in mind when he sings: "Love never dies, it will hold on more fierce than graves." The Hebrew word for love used by David in Psalm 23 v 6 is *chesed* (the "ch" is pronounced like the "ch" in the word *achtung*, and the syllables rhyme with "press" and "red"). It's the word used in the Old Testament to refer to God's special love for his covenant people. There's nothing in this universe better than being in covenant relationship with God, because of his *chesed*.

Part Two
The Seven Divine Covenants

Chapter 3

The Creational Covenant

"And it was very good" Genesis 1 v 31

According to a Celtic myth, the world was created when one of the gods was sacrificed by his rebellious children. His skull became the sky, and his blood the sea.

In another story, told by the Bushongo people of central Africa, a god called Bumba vomited up the sun after feeling a pain in his stomach. The sun then dried up the waters of the earth, causing land to emerge. Afterwards, still in pain, Bumba vomited up the moon and the stars.

In a creation myth from North America, Inktonmi, the god of the Assiniboine tribe, sent a muskrat to the bottom of the sea covering the world. The drowned body of the muskrat floated back to the surface, but before its death it had gathered soil in its claws. From that soil Inktonmi made land.[12]

One thing those myths have in common is the touch-and-go nature of creation. It's the chance outcome of a family feud, or a stomach pain, or a rodent's ocean dive. When we turn to the Bible's true account of creation, we find that God is in complete control of proceedings. Rather than making things up along the way, he's executing a plan. As soon as he's created the first human beings, he presents them with a detailed covenant.

The word "covenant" isn't used in the creation account itself, but it is used in a later Bible passage looking back on events in the Garden of Eden. God says: "Like Adam, they have broken the covenant – they were unfaithful to me" (Hosea 6 v 7).[13] What's more, there's clear evidence of an agreement establishing a relationship with life or death consequences. We can tell there's a relationship in place between God and mankind because God comes to the garden to enjoy Adam and Eve's company (Genesis 3 v 8-9). And there's no doubt that a life or death condition is attached to their friendship:

Genesis 2 v 16-17

The Lord God commanded the man, "You are free to eat from any tree in the garden; but you must not eat from the tree of the knowledge of good and evil, for when you eat of it you will surely die."

If Adam and Eve disobey this command, they'll be put to death. If they keep it, they'll live. In this way a covenant is established at the time of creation.[14] But there's more to the creational covenant than just the forbidden fruit. God sets out several other instructions that should also be seen as part of the covenant offer.

Work

Adam and Eve are given a job to do: "God blessed them and said to them, 'Be fruitful and increase in number; fill the earth and subdue it'" (Genesis 1 v 28). This tells us that the world God created, although "very good" (verse 31), isn't the finished article. It needs subduing. It's designed to reach its optimum state through responsible cultivation by humanity (see also Genesis 2 v 5). We could say that

God's world is delivered to mankind in flat-packed form, requiring further assembly.

This point is repeated elsewhere in the Bible. In Psalm 104, for example, certain features of creation require mankind's contribution:

Psalm 104 v 14-15
[The LORD] makes grass grow for the cattle,
and plants for man to cultivate –
bringing forth food from the earth:
wine that gladdens the heart of man,
oil to make his face shine,
and bread that sustains his heart.

We can tell from the psalm that God wants his world to contain wine, oil and bread. But he's set everything up so that human labour is part of the production process. To get those things, mankind will need to work at tasks such as pruning, gathering, crushing, picking, pressing, sowing, harvesting, threshing, winnowing, grinding, and baking. In a similar way, the temple commissioned by God (1 Kings 5 v 5) requires the mining of gold, the quarrying of stones and the felling of trees. The world comes flat-packed, and God commands mankind to assemble it. Work is therefore an essential feature of life.

It's important to notice that the decree to subdue the earth begins: "God blessed them". Work isn't something to grumble about; it's a blessing we should praise God for. As we shall see, work is cursed by God after the fall, which does make it harder and more troublesome. But all the same, the Bible continues to view work positively (see 2 Thessalonians 3 v 6-13). It's an aspect of the creational covenant that blesses us by giving us something to do that matters to God.

Marriage

Anyone wondering why marriage is an integral part of social life across all five continents can find the answer in the Bible's second chapter. It explains that marriage is God's answer to a problem. God says: "It is not good for the man to be alone. I will make a helper suitable for him" (Genesis 2 v 18). Many people assume on the basis of that verse that marriage is God's solution for loneliness. But that's to forget that Adam had God's company in the garden – he did not lack fellowship. There's a different reason why man's aloneness is the one thing considered "not good" during creation week. As Christopher Ash says in his book *Marriage*:

> *In the context of Genesis 1 humans are made to rule a world ... which will be out of control unless it is ruled. How may we fulfil this task? We ... need to "be fruitful and multiply" so that there will be sufficient human beings to exercise responsible dominion.*[15]

In other words, it's not good for Adam to be alone because it would be impossible for him to subdue the earth as a single man. But with a woman on the scene humanity can multiply, and so the job of ruling the earth becomes achievable. As the saying goes, many hands make light work.

God describes the woman's role as "helper" (sometimes translated "aid") to the man. This word is significant. It implies that the roles of husband and wife are different. It suggests that Adam is the one who should be leading the relationship. This interpretation seems to be confirmed when Adam is the one held responsible for the couple's disobedience in the garden (see Romans 5 v 12, 14, 19), even though it was Eve's idea (1 Timothy 2 v 14). The thought of leadership within marriage might set off alarm bells for some readers, but we shouldn't equate *leadership* with *exploitation*. Biblical leadership is servant-hearted (Mark 10 v 42-45). It prioritises the welfare of the one being led. And understanding marriage in this way certainly doesn't mean that women have less value than men. Both the man and the woman are created "in the image of God" (Genesis 1 v 27), which gives them equal worth. What's more, as Sharon James points out, the role of helper is heaven-touched:

Many women today instinctively cringe when they hear that we are to be helpers. In our day the word carries overtones of a junior assistant, one who is relegated to an inferior position. An effective antidote to that misconception is to trace through the Psalms for references to God as helper. God reveals himself to be the helper of the poor, the needy, the distressed, the fatherless, the underprivileged, the oppressed and the homeless.[16]

So when a wife helps her husband, she imitates God. Her role is one that God himself, while not appointed to it, is willing to carry out.

The woman is created by God out of the man's body:

Genesis 2 v 21-22
The Lord God caused the man to fall into a deep sleep; and while he was sleeping, he took one of the man's ribs and closed up the place with flesh. Then the Lord God made a woman from the rib he had taken out of the man, and he brought her to the man.

This method of creating the woman leads to a powerful desire for reunification. Verse 24 refers back to verse 22 when it says: "*For this reason* a man will leave his father and mother and be united to his wife, and they will become one flesh."[17] The ribcage longs to find his missing rib. The rib will not rest until she's reunited with her ribcage. So it's no surprise when single men are filled with desire for the female body, and single women long for a man to hold them. They're ribcages and ribs in search of one another.

The "missing rib" principle also explains why marriage can't be between two people of the same sex.[18] Only a rib cage and a rib can be reunited. Two ribs, or two rib cages can't become "one flesh". Marriage to more than one person is another distortion of the rib/ribcage principle established in the garden. And divorce is also ruled out on the same basis: Jesus looks back to Genesis 2 v 24 when he says: "Therefore what God has joined together, let man not separate" (Mark 10 v 6-9).[19]

So the blueprint for marriage introduced in Eden still applies today. However, the new covenant has brought in a major change of attitude to singleness. In Old Testament times remaining single was effectively a rejection of God's creational command to be fruitful and fill the earth. There was no place for voluntary celibacy (see Judges 11 v 38-40 and Isaiah 4 v 1). But now God's people are encouraged to consider lifelong singleness. Clyde Ervine sums up the difference in outlook:

> *In Jesus' new order, the status of marriage changes and the status of singleness changes with it ... marriage in the New Testament is neither obligatory, nor singleness shameful. Accordingly, Jesus, Paul, and many early church leaders remained single. Their singleness,*

as with others' marriages, was understood as a perfectly legitimate way to live out the Christian life.[20]

In *Bridget Jones' Diary*, Helen Fielding coined the phrase "Smug Marrieds" to describe the way married thirty-somethings sometimes appear to the thirty-somethings who are still single (like Bridget). But the New Testament doesn't share Bridget Jones' assumption that marriage is best. In fact, Paul sounds rather like a "Smug Singleton" when he says of his singleness: "I wish that all men were as I am" (1 Corinthians 7 v 7). He goes on: "Now to the unmarried and the widows I say: It is good for them to stay unmarried, as I am" (verse 8). Paul explains his enthusiasm for singleness later in the chapter (see verses 28, 32-34).

For most believers, however, the powerful desire for reunification with a rib or ribcage means that marriage is wise. Paul acknowledges this in 1 Corinthians 7 v 2: "Since there is so much immorality, each man should have his own wife, and each woman her own husband." He makes the same point in 1 Thessalonians 4 v 3-4.[21]

Guarding against sexual immorality might not seem like a very romantic reason to get married, but Paul is being realistic. His teaching makes sense when we remember that we're either incomplete ribcages or missing ribs, so our bodies cry out for sex. Remaining single requires special giftedness (1 Corinthians 7 v 7).[22]

But what about those people who feel they lack any kind of gift for staying single and yet currently have no opportunity to get married? This difficult predicament calls for trust, because God *can* provide us with the strength and wisdom we need to be content whatever our circumstances (Philippians 4 v 12-13, James 1 v 2-5).

The Sabbath day

God has already blessed mankind once (Genesis 1 v 28). His next blessing concerns the final day of creation week: "And God blessed the seventh day and made it holy, because on it he rested from all the work of creating that he had done" (Genesis 2 v 3). This is the first ever Sabbath day. We can be sure of that, despite the absence of the word, because Exodus 20 v 11 describes the seventh day of creation as the Sabbath: "For in six days the LORD made the heavens and the earth, the sea, and all that is in them, but he rested on the seventh day. Therefore the LORD blessed the Sabbath day and made it holy." The Sabbath is a day for Adam and Eve to "be refreshed" (Exodus 23 v 12). It will keep them from growing weary and stale.

Throughout this book we'll need to figure out which clauses from past covenants endure all the way through to our own covenant, and which don't. Some Christians have argued that the Sabbath no longer applies in our period of salvation history. There's not room in this book to go into the debate fully.[23] But the presence of the Sabbath in the Garden of Eden should persuade Bible readers that it's a lasting design feature of our world, like other creational ordinances (see 1 Timothy 2 v 11-13). In the New Testament Jesus upholds the Sabbath and makes it clear that he expects his followers to keep it after his departure (see Matthew 24 v 20). J.C. Ryle, the nineteenth-century Christian leader, puts it well:

I find Jesus speaking eleven times on the subject of the Sabbath, but it is always to correct the superstitious additions which the Pharisees had made to the Law of Moses about observing it, and never to deny the holiness of the day. He no more abolishes the

Sabbath than a man destroys a house when he cleans off the moss or weeds from its roof.[24]

After Jesus' resurrection the Sabbath day seems to switch from the seventh day of the week (Saturday) to the first day of the week (Sunday), because the early church begins meeting together on Sundays rather than Saturdays (Acts 20 v 7; 1 Corinthians 16 v 2).[25]

The forbidden tree

It's impossible not to be attracted to life under the creational covenant, as described in the opening chapters of Genesis. Adam and Eve enjoy the pleasures of marriage. There's satisfying labour to be done – cultivating the earth without any trouble from weeds or pests. And every week they have one full day of refreshment. They're situated in the Garden of Eden, where the trees are "pleasing to the eye and good for food" (Genesis 2 v 9). And as long as they have access to the tree of life, they'll live forever (Genesis 3 v 22). On top of all these blessings, they enjoy the presence of their Creator God – according to Genesis 3 v 8, he walks with them in the garden.

But Adam and Eve aren't locked in to this state of affairs. Should they wish to take it, there's an exit route:

Genesis 2 v 17
And the LORD God commanded the man, "You are free to eat from any tree in the garden; but you must not eat from the tree of the knowledge of good and evil, for when you eat of it you will surely die."

This presents them with an alternative to the creational covenant. They can reject it.

We shouldn't view the forbidden tree as a negative feature of the Garden of Eden, like a creepy haunted house that all the children of the neighbourhood hurry past. Covenants treat people as responsible individuals because they require the willing agreement of those taking part. Without the forbidden tree that kind of covenant relationship with God wouldn't be possible for Adam and Eve. They would have nothing to agree to, because they'd have no alternative to life in the garden with God. But the presence of the forbidden tree allows them to affirm their commitment to the covenant. Every time they pass it they can say to themselves: "Let's never eat from that tree, because the relationship we've got with God is so good." In this way the tree makes a consenting covenant relationship possible. Such a relationship is infinitely richer than sharing God's company without any other option.

The tree promises to reward those who eat its fruit with the knowledge of good and evil. This can't mean knowing the difference between good and evil: Adam and Eve can already choose between obeying God (good) or rebelling against him (evil). Another misunderstanding is the idea that eating from the tree would give Adam and Eve the experience of good and evil. That must be wrong, because after they've eaten, God says: "The man has now become *like one of us*, knowing good and evil" (Genesis 3 v 22). God has no personal experience of sin – he "cannot be tempted by evil" (James 1 v 13) – and so the knowledge of good and evil must mean something else.

So what exactly does the tree offer? Later in the Bible, King Solomon prays: "Give your servant therefore an understanding mind to govern your people, that I may discern between good and evil" (1 Kings 3 v 9, ESV). Solomon looks to God for help in working out what's right and what's wrong. He's saying to God: "Knowing good and evil is your department". The tree says the same thing *to human beings*. To eat from it isn't just to break one of God's commands. It's to reject God's right to lay down any commands. If the tree had an advertising tagline, it would be: "Your Life – Your Rules".

Life lessons

- The twentieth-century poet Philip Larkin was not a fan of work, according to his poem "Toads":

Why should I let the toad work
Squat on my life?
Can't I use my wit as a pitchfork
And drive the brute off?

Six days of the week it soils
With its sickening poison –
Just for paying a few bills!
That's out of proportion …

Ah, were I courageous enough
To shout Stuff your pension!
But I know, all too well, that's the stuff
That dreams are made on.

In a later poem, "Toads Revisited", Larkin admits that work does at least stave off boredom and loneliness. It ends with the bleak lines:

Give me your arm, old toad;
Help me down Cemetery Road.

The Bible's view of work is so different! **God has given us the exciting challenge of taming (not trashing) the world.** There are raw materials throughout creation ready to be put to good use. As we do so, we're fulfilling the Creator's purposes for his world. This dignifies work. God wants meals to be well cooked, classes well taught, websites well designed, roads well maintained, babies well nurtured, and countries well governed – in short, every task that contributes to the positive development of creation matters to him. God's creational mandate to subdue the earth has never been revoked. The new covenant doesn't tug us away from our roles in that project; it urges us to carry them out with fresh vigour (see 1 Corinthians 7 v 17-24; Colossians 3 v 23; and 2 Thessalonians 3 v 10-12). Some of us, however, will be set apart to serve God's people full-time (see for example 1 Corinthians 9 v 14). In a sense that work is dedicated more to the new creation (of which believers are the firstfruits according to James 1 v 18) than this present world. But we shouldn't think of those believers as more spiritual or zealous than the ones doing regular creational labour. God has commissioned both creational work and new creation work, he wants both to be done, and the distribution of personnel is up to him (Acts 20 v 28; Ephesians 4 v 11; John 3 v 27). Each of us needs to discern how we fit in to God's commissioning. Needless to say, every Christian is expected to do at least some new creation work (1 Peter 2 v 5, 9).

- *"Six days you shall labour and do all your work,"* God says at Sinai, looking back to the creational covenant, *"but the seventh day is a Sabbath to the LORD your God"* (Exodus

20 v 9-10). **We need to trust in God's creational 6-on-1-off pattern and apply it to our lives.** That's not to say we should insist on doing our regular job for six days a week instead of the normal five! Getting the whole weekend off, as many of us do in the west, is a bonus. It releases a day for other kinds of productivity: family projects, building relationships with non-Christians, serving the church, or getting through all the tasks and chores that life inevitably generates. As a result it's much easier to keep the Sabbath clear.

• What does keeping the Sabbath mean in practice? Maybe it brings to mind bored kids wearing starchy clothes in Victorian sitting rooms, listening to the clock tick. It's true the Sabbath has been badly misapplied in the past. People seem to have forgotten that Jesus said: "The Sabbath was made for man, not man for the Sabbath" (Mark 2 v 27) – in other words **the Sabbath was made for our benefit, not for the day's honour.** Jesus' easygoing attitude gives us a certain amount of freedom in the way we fill the day.[26]

However, we do find two headline principles in the Bible that keep us from misusing the Sabbath. One is the need for refreshment: "On the seventh day do not work, so that your ox and your donkey may rest and the slave born in your household, and the alien as well, may be refreshed" (Exodus 23 v 12). In the original Hebrew there are three different verbs to do with resting in that one verse – God wants his people to get the message. Subduing the earth calls for energetic output, and we need an "energy-in" day to recharge. Doing things that leave us exhausted would therefore be against the spirit of the day.

The other principle is that the Sabbath is "holy to the LORD" (Exodus 31 v 15). It may be a day off work, but it's not a day off from loving God. The Sabbath gives us some welcome extra time for our relationship with him. We can spend longer than usual reading his word and praying. And we can draw near to him through gathering with other believers, something that's happened throughout history on the Sabbath day. William Wilberforce is one great figure from Christian history who knew his need for the Sabbath. After a week of political upheaval in 1801 he wrote in his journal on Sunday night: "Blessed be God for the day of rest and religious occupation wherein earthly things assume their true size. Ambition is stunted, and I hope my affections in some degree rise to things above."[27]

- Marriage, God's ancient invention, still appeals to people throughout the world. The children's film *Shrek* may have reinvented the traditional fairy tale when a kiss from Princess Fiona's "true love" turned her into a green ogress – but she still got married at the end. But the world's current attitude to marriage is by no means biblical in every way. **Believers need to be counter-cultural in sticking with God's plan for marriage.** This will mean keeping sex for marriage; seeking only a Christian marriage partner (see 1 Corinthians 7 v 39); and staying married. An alternative that's even more counter-cultural is lifelong celibacy, as modelled by Jesus and Paul. They were able to give more of their time and energy to the cause of God's kingdom because of their singleness – and who would say their lives were not lived to the max?

  In the New Testament we're told that marriage is

a picture of the relationship between Jesus and the church. Paul quotes Genesis 2 v 24: "For this reason a man will leave his father and mother and be united to his wife, and the two will become one flesh", and then he says, "I am talking about Christ and the church" (Ephesians 5 v 32). Jesus' desire for his people was so strong – despite our sinfulness – that he left the courts of heaven to make the church his bride, at the cost of his own life. Are you receptive to his love?

- **The creational covenant helps us understand why non-Christians stand condemned before God even if they haven't heard about Jesus:**

Isaiah 24 v 5-6

The earth is defiled by its people;
they have disobeyed the laws, violated the statutes
and broken the everlasting covenant.
Therefore a curse consumes the earth;
its people must bear their guilt.

As children of Adam, made in God's image, all mankind inherits the covenantal obligation to rule over the earth in a beneficial way. Yet instead we stand guilty of defiling it – which is more than just a matter of environmental damage, although that's certainly part of it. Humanity is wired to know that things such as murder, adultery, theft and lying are evil (Romans 2 v 14-15). And yet each one of us defiles the earth by doing those very things in our different ways (see Matthew 5 v 21-37). We even hurt the people we love the most. In harming other people, we harm the world. God is proved right when he speaks, and justified when he judges (Psalm 51 v 4), because we all violate the creational covenant.

- **Meditating on Eden ought to fill believers with longing for what God has in store for us.** That's because there's a real sense in which the world to come will be Eden restored.[28] But it will be even better than Eden, since there's no possibility that it will end. Although it was good for Adam and Eve to have the forbidden tree in the garden, because it enabled willing covenant relationship, it did open up the possibility of the fall. But in the book of Revelation's advance screening of the new heavens and the new earth, there's no sign of the "tree of the knowledge of good and evil". Those who take part in the new creation have already signalled their personal consent to the eternal covenant through faith in God's promises. Nothing will stop us enjoying God's presence for ever.

Chapter 4

The Covenant with Adam

"Through the obedience of the one man" Romans 5 v 19

The story so far

God wants to be in relationship with humanity. But that can only happen once a covenant has been put in place: an agreement establishing a relationship with life or death consequences. In the Garden of Eden, God's covenant offer included work, marriage and the Sabbath. Adam and Eve could reject the covenant by eating from the tree of the knowledge of good and evil. Life in the garden was "very good".

A covenant broken

In the Bible only two animals speak: Balaam's donkey, and the snake in the Garden of Eden. A rare event calls for an explanation. It seems that Satan takes possession of a snake's body so that he can speak with its split tongue.[29] As a result "the serpent was more crafty than any of the wild animals the LORD God had made" (Genesis 3 v 1). This craftiness is seen immediately:

Genesis 3 v 1
He said to the woman, "Did God really say, 'You must not eat from any tree in the garden?'"

Satan's question implies that God might be a killjoy, something Eve had probably never considered before. Maybe God can't be trusted to act in her and her husband's best interests. This puts Eve in the perfect zone for Satan's next play. Once she has explained that only one tree is outlawed, and eating its fruit would mean death, Satan says: "You will not surely die, for God knows that when you eat of it your eyes will be opened, and you will be like God, knowing good and evil" (3 v 4-5).

At this point Eve's physical sensations and personal longings come off the bench to join Satan's side: "The woman saw that the fruit of the tree was good for food and pleasing to the eye, and also desirable for gaining wisdom" (3 v 6). Everything is now urging her on: the advice of her new companion, her hunger, her delight in beauty, and her desire for wisdom. The only thing standing in her way is the word of God. But sometimes God's word can seem very flimsy and insignificant. Why should she worry about it? So she takes some of the fruit, and gives some to Adam, who's standing beside her (v 6), and they eat. One act of disobedience, with a horde of devastating consequences.

Eating from the forbidden tree triggers the punishment for covenant breaking: separation from God (Genesis 3 v 23-24) and death (3 v 19, 22). Adam and Eve have shared paradise with God, but now they're banished from Eden and will ultimately return to dust. The garden's entrance is barred by angels and a terrifying flaming sword (Genesis 3 v 24). A world that was once "very good" (Genesis 1 v 31) becomes a "valley of weeping" (Psalm 84 v 6, NLT).

A covenant offered

Satan had been lying. God says Adam and Eve *will* die because of what they've done. But he doesn't put them to death right away. And what happens next is stunning: God presents another covenant so that his relationship with mankind can continue outside Eden. Once again, although the word covenant isn't found in the passage, all the hallmarks of a covenant are present. There are terms of agreement offering mankind a way back to God. Those who accept the covenant will live (see Genesis 5 v 22-24; Hebrews 11 v 5), while those who ignore it will die.[30] The covenant with Adam promises that all is not lost, yet it also confirms the painful nature of life in a fallen world.

1. Future hope

God curses each of the participants in the rebellion against him. But in cursing the snake, he makes a three-part declaration that rekindles hope for humanity. The relevant verse, Genesis 3 v 15, has been called "the first gospel sermon that was ever delivered upon the surface of this earth."[31] It's central to the covenant with Adam, so we need to look at it closely. The verse predicts three separate battles:

[Battle #1]
I will put enmity between you and the woman...
[Battle #2]
...and between your offspring and hers...
[Battle #3]
...he will crush your head, and you will strike his heel.

People's attitude towards the eternal covenant is revealed by where they stand in these battles.

At first sight Battle #1, between Satan and Eve, might seem futile – after all, they're both cursed by God. What's to be gained when a couple of inmates stuck in the same cell take each other on? But there are two reasons why this battle isn't pointless.

First, it's a conflict provoked by God himself. He says: "I will put enmity between you and the woman". God must think there's real value to this fight or else he wouldn't start it. Second, the battles of Genesis 3 v 15 end with the fatal crushing of Satan. So Eve is on the winning side. She'll share in the spoils of victory. Elsewhere the Bible teaches that victory over Satan means victory over death (Hebrews 2 v 14-15).

Battle #2 in Genesis 3 v 15 is fought between Satan's offspring, and the woman's offspring. The Hebrew word translated "offspring" can refer to a group or an individual. Satan's offspring is generally viewed by the Bible as a group, which means in Battle #2 his offspring is best understood as an army rather than a single fighter. That would make the woman's offspring a group too, because otherwise the battle would be lopsided.

But who exactly are the troops in these two armies? The Bible says that Satan's children are regular human beings who do his will (John 8 v 44; 1 John 3 v 10). The other army must be people who take after the woman in resisting Satan. The conflict between Satan's offspring and the woman's offspring has continued throughout history (see for example Matthew 23 v 29-35, and Mark 13 v 13).

Battle #3 speaks of the final destruction of Satan. The "he" who'll crush Satan is one man representing the woman's offspring from Battle #2.[32] It's clear that all the credit for Satan's defeat should go to this victorious combatant in Battle #3. Without his decisive strike there would be no reason to think that the first two battles would end successfully. He supplies hope to the covenant with Adam.

instead of Abel, for Cain killed him"
In this second speech Eve hints at her
with Cain. He's guilty of murder so there's
he's both man and God. And Abel's now
crush the serpent either. Yet she's evidently
promise of Genesis 3 v 15 because she uses
spring" when talking about her latest boy.
her hopes to him. In this way Eve shows
covenant with Adam. She's holding on
of salvation through the future serpent-
one of her male descendants.[36]

Cain and Abel in Genesis 4 tells us more
the covenant with Adam. Cain presents
but God does not look with favour on his
4 v 5). Abel, on the other hand, presents an
that's well received (4 v 4). God's reaction to
might seem unfair because we're told: "Abel
Cain worked the soil" (4 v 2). So it looks as
offering is linked to their job. But clearly
for Cain's displeasing offering: God says
me "what is right" (4 v 7). The problem with
is that it's bloodless.[37] He's failed to grasp
always falls short of the standards required
with God. We can only stay in covenant
th God if a substitute receives the penalty
of us. Abel, unlike Cain, has understood that
eds to die in his place. Later on in the Bible
set out plainly: "It is the blood that makes
one's life" (Leviticus 17 v 11).

mple of the choice facing mankind in this
zone is the case of "**the two Lamechs**". Two
ed Lamech, respond very differently to God's
The first Lamech is found in Genesis 4:

He's single-handedly responsible for sustaining the eternal covenant.

But surely it's impossible for any child of the woman to be powerful enough to crush Satan? Adam and Eve couldn't conquer him when they were still innocent of sin in Eden. How much less likely to defeat him is anyone born after the fall?

During home assignment in Britain in 2008, a missionary called Daniel Moore spoke about his work with a tribe in Papua New Guinea, teaching them the Bible's message from Genesis onwards. Daniel said that when they reached the news of a promised saviour in Genesis 3 v 15, a tribesman called out: "He would have to be God!" It was one of their earliest sessions, but that tribesman had caught sight of a profound truth. No fallen human could ever defeat the devil. Verses such as Genesis 8 v 21 and 1 Kings 8 v 46 put that beyond doubt. The implication is inescapable: this promised redeemer descended from Eve will somehow be both man and God.

2. Present curse

Imagine a wooden building ruined by termites. Get rid of the termites and reconstruction can begin. Mankind's ruin came about because of Satan, but the covenant with Adam reveals that a saviour will destroy Satan, making reconstruction possible. So anyone on the conqueror's side can joyfully expect that the fall won't be permanent. But in the meantime, the location of the battles of Genesis 3 v 15 is a stricken world. Those who sign up to the covenant with Adam must patiently endure not only the fight with Satan and his offspring but also life under God's curse.

Both the woman and the man are cursed in their separate areas of responsibility. Eve must give birth to ensure the future arrival of mankind's saviour. She and her husband also need children to help them with the continuing obligation to subdue the earth. But carrying out this covenantal task will now mean agonising labour-pains (Genesis 3 v 16). What's more, her relationship with her husband is likely to be troubled from this point onwards. God says to her: "You will desire to control your husband, but he will rule over you" (Genesis 3 v 16, NLT).[33] Eve will instinctively want the leadership role that rightly belongs to Adam. His natural response, backed up by greater physical strength, will be to enforce her submission. God is warning Eve about the marital tension that's likely to come.

The man is also cursed. From now on Adam's daily work will be blighted by a curse on the land (Genesis 3 v 17-19). Thorns and thistles will hinder his efforts. Cultivating the earth will leave him drenched in sweat, with blistered feet and calloused hands.

All the natural disasters that afflict the world are contained in seed-form in this curse on the land. It's at this point that the world is "subjected to frustration" and put into "bondage to decay" (Romans 8 v 20-21). Drought, pests, flooding, earthquakes, volcanic eruptions, hurricanes and all kinds of sickness and disability date back to God's curse upon the world at the time of the fall. This is the Bible's explanation of "the problem of pain". The world was justly subjected to punishment as a result of man's rebellion. If God had cushioned us from the consequences of our sin, how would we have known our need for him?

A covenant accepted

The covenant with Adam takes up only a few pages of Scripture. But it governs how people relate to God for at least 1500 years, judging by the genealogy of Genesis chapter

5. In the lang
this book, the
lengthy part o
time some peo
keep the fires (
studies will hel
sign up to the c

We tend to l
Jezebel, Athalia
real change in he
To start with, a
the starring role
he'll put enmity l
listen to his forke

Then in Genesi
speeches. The firs
literal translation
Yahweh."[34] She d
child, which qual
But more than tha
be God-come-dov
"Jehovah", is God'
Bibles translate Yah
founder of Souther
the following helpf

She had believed the
fulfilment, and had le
Jehovah with the expec
only did she believe th
she expected his appea

Later in the chapter

another offspring
(verse 25, ESV).
disappointment
no chance that
dead, so he can't
still trusting in th
the key word "of
She's transferred
how to accept th
to God's promis
crushing work o

The account o
about accepting
crops to God, b
offering (Genesi
animal sacrifice
these offerings
kept flocks, and
if their choice
that's no excus
Cain has not do
Cain's offering
that humanity
for fellowship
relationship w
for sin instead
a substitute ne
this principle
atonement for

Another ex
salvation time
men, both nar
covenant offe

Genesis 4 v 23-24

Lamech said to his wives,
"Adah and Zillah, listen to me;
wives of Lamech, hear my words.
I have killed a man for wounding me,
a young man for injuring me.
If Cain is avenged seven times,
Then Lamech seventy-seven times."

This Lamech is Cain's great-great-great grandson, and he goes into the family business – homicide. After murdering a young man, he excuses himself by distorting an ancient promise made by God to his ancestor, Cain. When Cain killed Abel, God condemned him to live as "a restless wanderer" (Genesis 4 v 12). But he assured Cain that anyone who killed him would "suffer vengeance seven times over" (4 v 15). Lamech, however, twists this promise to Cain into his own personal license to kill. Instead of remembering the terms of God's covenant, he's holding on to a minor message from God with no power to save.

The other Lamech is the great-great-great-great-great grandson of Seth, Cain's younger brother. Like Eve, he makes a comment that is full of faith at the birth of a baby boy: "He will comfort us in the labour and painful toil of our hands caused by the ground the LORD has cursed" (Genesis 5 v 29). This statement shows that someone has told Lamech what happened at the beginning of history. He clearly believes that the land has not always been cursed. What's more, Lamech trusts that help is coming. Like Eve before him, he voices his hope that his own son will be the one who'll take the curse away.

It's worth looking at one final case study, which must have given tremendous confidence to the believers of that time. We're told in Genesis chapter 5 that "**Enoch** walked with God; then he was no more, because God took him away" (verse 24). This information about Enoch comes in the middle of a long family tree. There's a bleak catchphrase in that chapter: "and then he died". It's said of every member of the genealogy *apart from Enoch*. We're not told where exactly God takes him, but it's impossible to avoid the conclusion that he does not die (this is later confirmed by Hebrews 11 v 5). What could be more encouraging to people trusting in the covenant with Adam? Enoch proves that death can be overcome. The fall is not irreversible.

These case studies clarify what it means to accept the covenant with Adam. Eve and the second Lamech take us to the heart of the covenant: they demonstrate trust in the promise of a coming saviour. Enoch exemplifies walking with God, resisting Satan, in sharp contrast to Cain and the first Lamech. But no one stays perfectly committed to covenant relationship with God, and so believers offer animal sacrifices, as modelled by Abel. Enoch's escape from death strengthens hope that the covenant really does lead to eternal life in God's presence.

Life lessons

- **The Bible's Jesus-centredness should be reflected in our own Bible teaching and the teaching we choose to sit beneath.** Already, after just two pages, the Bible is urging readers to look out for a coming champion who'll defeat Satan. He'll be human – a descendant of the woman – but also divine. God himself will come to save his people. A classical symphony generally has a principal melody, known as the "melodic line", to which the orchestra keeps returning. From the covenant with Adam onwards, the Bible's melodic line is the promise that a saviour is coming. It's the beautiful, surging tune that keeps recurring. So we need to make sure that the Bible teaching we receive and deliver never moves too far from Jesus.

- **The covenant with Adam teaches us that believers must expect conflict with non-Christians.** We belong to opposing armies, according to Battle #2 of Genesis 3 v 15. As Paul says to Timothy: "Everyone who wants to live a godly life in Christ Jesus will be persecuted" (2 Timothy 3 v 12). This explains why Jesus says we should rejoice when we face persecution (Matthew 5 v 11-12). Experiencing hostility from people because of our faith is a sign that we're on the winning side. That's a cause for joy even if the abuse is bitter and the wounds are deep. It's a joy that strengthens us to pray for those currently opposing us (Matthew 5 v 44).

- The two armies of Battle #2 are distinguished from each other by their attitude to Satan. One side opposes him, while the other gives in to his temptations without resistance. Which army do you belong to? How do you respond to the temptations rolled in your direction by the devil? Do you consider the word of God feeble and unimportant, as Eve did in the garden? **By the power of God's Spirit we must fight the temptation to disobey God** (Romans 8 v 13). That means more than simply praying for the Spirit's help, although that's vital. The Spirit works through God's word, which is his sword (Ephesians 6 v 17), and so we need to expose ourselves to Scripture. Reading the Bible daily – perhaps just for ten minutes – is one good way to do that. Another is bringing God's word into our conversations with Christian friends, sharing the truth with one another in love (Ephesians 4 v 15, 29). It's easier to obey God's word when it's fresh in your mind.

If you know something of this struggle against temptation, you should be encouraged. It's a sign that God has stepped into your life to "put enmity" between you and the devil. It proves the reality of God's work within.

- The travel supplements in the weekend newspapers often give the impression that we can escape the fall in this life. Their reports of holiday destinations portray a world without hardship. While it's true that God allows us to counteract the fall (through modern medicine for example, and labour-saving machinery), the world is still under judgment. We can't travel away from the world's fallenness, no matter how much spending power we might have. But the covenant with Adam tells us that our saviour will bring about an end to the fall. **As we experience the difficulties of life in a cursed world, we should fix our eyes on the glory to come**. Focusing day after day on that future will help us keep on walking with God like Enoch.

- **Only Jesus offers hope for humanity.** Paul makes this clear in Romans chapter 5 when he divides the whole of mankind into two groups. One is led into sin by Adam, the other given grace, justification, righteousness and life through Jesus: "For just as through the disobedience of the one man the many were made sinners, so also through the obedience of the one man the many will be made righteous" (Romans 5 v 19). If you know that you're still "in Adam", take this opportunity to make Jesus your figurehead and from now on live "in Christ" (1 Corinthians 15 v 22).

- The contest between the woman's descendant and Satan in Battle #3 is a vicious death brawl. Humanity's representative reacts with courage and power to stamp down on the serpent's head, crushing its skull. But in the process of the tussle, the snake succeeds in striking its adversary's heel with its poisonous fangs. Our champion's victory was won at the great cost of his own life. **Jesus' willingness to die in our place should stir up our thankfulness.** As he himself says, "Greater love has no-one than this, that he lay down his life for his friends" (John 15 v 13).

Chapter 5

The Covenant with Noah

"Never again will I curse the ground" Genesis 8 v 21

The story so far

In Eden God decreed that Adam and Eve should rule over and cultivate the whole world. Through marriage they would increase in number to achieve this. God also set aside one day a week for refreshment. However, mankind rejected this covenant by submitting to Satan and eating from the forbidden tree. Adam and Eve faced the penalty for covenant violation. But God gave them hope through a second covenant, which promised a champion who would defeat Satan. Covenant keepers believed that promise, resisted temptation, and offered sacrifices to atone for sin.

Introducing the covenant with Noah

The covenants are God's way of structuring his salvation plan. The Bible makes that easy for us to see, because each covenant comes at a time when God's people experience a dramatic new beginning. That's obvious with the creational covenant, but it's also true of the covenant with Adam. It's made when Adam and Eve stumble away from Eden into a changed world. The covenant with Noah also accompanies a new start for the people of God. When Peter looks back on the world before the flood, he says: *"The world of that time* was deluged and destroyed" (2 Peter 3 v 6). So once the floodwaters have receded, the ramp of Noah's ark leads down to a new world. The survivors of the flood have to start from scratch, and in that needy situation God presents them with another covenant.

Destruction delivered

The eternal covenant is God's offer of relationship. In the lead-up to the flood we discover just how little that offer matters to mankind:

Genesis 6 v 5-7

The LORD saw how great man's wickedness on the earth had become, and that every inclination of the thoughts of his heart was only evil all the time. The LORD was grieved that he had made man on the earth, and his heart was filled with pain. So the LORD said, "I will wipe mankind, whom I have created, from the face of the earth – men and animals, and creatures that move along the ground, and birds of the air – for I am grieved that I have made them."

From dawn to night the people of that time pay no attention to God. Their hearts are never motivated by the desire to please him, which means they're in a state of constant rebellion. A sports coach making notes during a match might scrawl a line or two next to each player's name: "Quick, hard-working, but clumsy"; or "Doesn't seem to want the ball"; or "Talented, but not a team player". In the passage above we get to look over God's shoulder to see his note on humanity: "Only evil all the time". The assessment couldn't be more negative. But God is well-placed to reach that verdict because he observes hidden motives. What God hopes to see within mankind is a passionate desire for him to get the glory that is rightly his. But the divine ultrasound carried out in Genesis 6 v 5 shows that human hearts naturally long for God to get lost.

God responds by deciding to "wipe mankind ... from the face of the earth" (Genesis 6 v 7). His chosen method of destruction is the flood. It's the foremost example in all history of God's hostility towards rebellious mankind.

The flood brings to mind colourful murals on kindergarten walls. We visualise happy pairs of giraffes and elephants heading towards a cosy ark. That mental picture only tells one side of the story. We mustn't forget the dark terror of the day the waters came. Jesus helps us:

Matthew 24 v 38-39

For in the days before the flood, people were eating and drinking, marrying and giving in marriage, up to the day Noah entered the ark; and they knew nothing about what would happen until the flood came and took them all away.

We can imagine the scene at one of the weddings Jesus mentions, in the moments before "all the springs of the great deep burst forth and the floodgates of the heavens were opened" (Genesis 7 v 11). The bride and groom have just cut the cake. They look into each other's eyes, glowing with pleasure. The best man is skimming through his speech, wondering if he should drop the unflattering story about the groom from the camping trip last summer. Some children are chasing each other round the tables.

When the first drops of rain start to fall, there's a general murmur of surprise. After all, the dry season began several weeks ago and the wedding was timed so they could enjoy the festivities in the sunshine. Suddenly there's water everywhere, surging across the land and coming down in torrents from above. It only takes a moment for people's thoughts to shift from their sodden clothes to a cold fear for their lives. People clamber on tables but the water quickly chases after them. The last sounds they hear are screams, and the last things they see are the thrashing limbs of their fellow wedding guests, desperately trying to swim to safety.

But beyond the scenes of panic a huge wooden ark floats serenely. Inside are eight people, protected by God from his floodwaters. After a year and seventeen days on board ship, Noah and his wife and their sons and daughters-in-law walk down the ark's gangway onto dry land. Given humanity's track record, what reason could God have for saving these eight people? Just as the flood demonstrates God's anger and severity, so the ark reveals his love. If all mankind had drowned in the flood, Eve's serpent-conquering descendant would never have been born. But through God's mercy, humanity does survive the flood. Covenant history can keep moving forward.

Preservation Promised

In February 2009, the Arthur Rylah Institute for Environmental Research warned that just twenty Christmas Island pipistrelle bats remained in existence. The future of the species depended on those twenty bats, each one only an inch or so long.[38] After the flood the human race is similarly vulnerable – its future rests on eight people. But the covenant God makes with Noah guarantees the safety of humanity. Everything to do with the covenant speaks of preservation. In this way it reflects God's loving determination to set apart a people for himself.

1. Safety from savagery

Genesis 9 v 1-2

Then God blessed Noah and his sons, saying to them, "Be fruitful and increase in number and fill the earth. The fear and dread of you will fall on all the beasts of the earth and all the birds of the air, upon every creature that moves along the ground, and upon all the fish of the sea; they are given into your hands."

We've grown so used to our security among the world's creatures that it takes a film like Alfred Hitchcock's *The Birds* to get us to imagine how different things could be. The film explores what would happen if flocks of birds began attacking people. It's famous for having none of the unnerving music that horror movies usually rely on. Instead it builds suspense through the sound of flapping wings.

The covenant with Noah explains why the scenario of *The Birds* has never actually taken place. God graciously restrains the feathered and furred armies from assaulting humanity. He causes the "fear and dread" of mankind to fall upon them. While picking a fight with certain creatures remains inadvisable, it's true to say that humanity has only very rarely been driven away by "the birds of the air" or "the beasts of the earth".

As John Calvin points out, God must have been protecting the human race in this way ever since the fall:

After the fall of man, the beasts were endued with new ferocity ... and if God did not wonderfully restrain their fierceness, the human race would be utterly destroyed.[39]

But it's at this point in salvation history, rather than straight after the fall, that God puts his protection on record.

2. Safety through severity

Genesis 9 v 6
Whoever sheds the blood of man,
by man shall his blood be shed;
for in the image of God
has God made man. [See also verse 5.]

As history demonstrates over and over again, humanity also needs protection from itself. Man can be as brutal towards man as the fiercest wild beast. At Auschwitz, one of the Nazi death camps, there's a sculpted plaque showing naked, skeletal figures beneath the words *"Homo Homini"*. It's a shortened version of the Latin saying: *"Lupus est homo homini"*, which means, "Man to man is a wolf". This clause of the covenant with Noah is designed to restrain mankind's violent nature. It sets down a judicial principle that anyone who commits murder should be put to death. This severe sentence will help to preserve those made in the image of God.

Christians disagree on whether this covenant clause endures all the way through to our own new covenant era. One argument for its enduring nature is that Paul appears to endorse the death penalty in Romans 13 v 3-4: "The one in authority … does not bear the sword for nothing. He is God's servant, an agent of wrath to bring punishment on the wrongdoer." (In the Bible "the sword" is shorthand for death.) If that's a correct interpretation of Paul's comment, it would suggest that Christians should support this legal principle. One man who would have welcomed the protection springing from capital punishment is a retired policeman called Gordon Law, author of the following letter to UK newspaper *The Times*:

Sir, I disagree that there is inadequate evidence that capital punishment acts as a deterrent. As a police officer, while trying to arrest some burglars, during the fight one of them came behind me and stabbed me in the back, the knife passing through my spine and leaving me paralysed.

At his court appearance he admitted attempting to murder me, giving the reason that, had I arrested him, he would go to prison for a long time because of his previous long criminal record. If, however, he murdered me he would either get clean away with it or if he was arrested for the murder he would only go to prison, the same as if I had arrested him for the burglary. His twisted logic was correct because he was sentenced to ten years, ten years and six months, with the three sentences to run concurrent, and was released after serving only four years and ten months.

Perhaps, if he had considered that he might have been hanged if caught for murder, then he may not have attempted to murder me.
("Capital Punishment", The Times, *September 21, 2009)*

The facts seem to bear out his argument: since the abolition of capital punishment in Britain in 1965, the murder rate has more than doubled.[40] Whether or not the death penalty clause of the covenant with Noah still applies today, the need to protect mankind from mankind is just as great as ever.

3. Safety from storms

Genesis 9 v 13-15

I have set my rainbow in the clouds, and it will be the sign of the covenant between me and the earth. Whenever I bring clouds over the earth and the rainbow appears in the clouds, I will remember my covenant between me and you and all living creatures of every kind. Never again will the waters become a flood to destroy all life.

Imagine being one of the eight people coming down out of the ark after the flood. What would go through your mind the first time you saw drops of rain speckling the ground? The last time it rained all the people you had ever known were drowned, apart from the others on the ark. Your pulse rate would double and the palms of your hand would gather icy sweat. No wonder God tells Noah time after time that the flood will never happen again (Genesis 8 v 21, 22; 9 v 11, 15). God backs up this promise with an extraordinary sign: the rainbow (9 v 13). It will be spread out among the clouds that recently brought such destruction. The rainbow is designed to reassure humanity that history will never be cut short by another flood.

In Hebrew the word for rainbow is exactly the same as the word for "bow"– the weapon used to fire lethal arrows. The bow set in the clouds points in God's direction. It's his way of saying that he'll take an arrow himself before breaking his promise never to flood the world again (9 v 14-16). This is a reminder that covenants aren't one-way traffic. God makes it clear that the penalty for covenant failure applies to him just as much as to mankind. When God makes a covenant, he's prepared to put his own life on the line. It's remarkable to see this so soon in Scripture. Far from being alien to the Old Testament, the possibility of the death of God is raised in its earliest pages.

And perhaps there's still further meaning to be found in the God-ward direction of the bow in the clouds. Mankind will inevitably return to wickedness after the flood, so it won't be long before destruction is deserved all over again. Yet God insists this will never happen (8 v 21). How can a holy God commit himself to the preservation of a sinful race, especially given the covenantal requirement for death after transgression? The only explanation is that God himself is planning to pay the price for mankind's sin. In this way the rainbow of the covenant with Noah could be seen as a visual prophecy of the cross. God knows that the arrow of the covenant curse will tear his body, not because he'll break his promise to Noah, but because mankind will fall short of the covenant's terms and thereby deserve death. Preserving humanity while upholding the covenant can only be achieved through the sacrificial death of God in mankind's place. So it's entirely fitting, in the book of Revelation, that a rainbow encircles the throne of "a Lamb, looking as if it had been slain" (Revelation 4 v 3; 5 v 6).

4. Safety through sacrifice

Genesis 9 v 4
But you must not eat meat that has its lifeblood still in it.

God's people need a substitute to pay the penalty for their sin by dying in their place. At this stage in salvation history, animals serve that purpose. The key moment is when the lifeblood pours out from the sacrificed animal, signifying its death. When something serves a noble purpose, it should be treated with respect. The Queen's grandchildren shouldn't take her coronation crown to a fancy-dress party. In the same way, given blood's importance in the sacrificial system, it wouldn't be right for Noah to eat the blood of animals. As God says later in the Bible: "I will set my face against that person who eats blood and will cut him off from his people. For the life of a creature is in the blood, and I have given it to you to make atonement for yourselves ... it is the blood that makes atonement for one's life" (Leviticus 17 v 10-11).

God's ban on eating blood reminds Noah of the import–

ance of the sacrificial system. It offers him eternal safety, because if a substitute receives the punishment for sin in his place, he'll be spared death. The problem, however, is that none of the animals sacrificed by Noah are suitable substitutes. Their blood is not effective for taking away sin (see Hebrews 10 v 4). But the blood of a sacrificed animal does function as a signpost towards better blood that's coming: the blood of Jesus, "poured out for many" (Matthew 26 v 28). A signpost to London isn't the same thing as London itself, but people who make use of it show that London is their goal. When Noah offers animal sacrifices, he's showing that he knows his need for forgiveness. He's taking advantage of the means provided for dealing with sin in his time zone of salvation history. God will honour that through "the sacrifice of the body of Jesus Christ once for all" (Hebrews 10 v 10; see also 9 v 15).

Life lessons

- As we saw in chapter two, when a past covenant is built into later covenants, some of its clauses might drop away. Those terms of agreement are then no longer necessary for relationship with God. So the former covenants are like walnuts – made up of both husk and kernel. We need to work out which parts are discarded like the husk, and which are preserved like the kernel. We've seen that, in the covenant with Noah, animal sacrifices were God's appointed means for making atonement. Now that Jesus' blood has been offered, there's no further need for animal sacrifices, or for the prohibition on eating the blood of animals.[41] **We should rejoice in our privileged position in salvation history**: God has provided us with one perfect sacrifice, "offered for all time" (Hebrews 10 v 12). This is infinitely better than "the same sacrifices repeated endlessly year after year" (Hebrews 10 v 1).

- **There's great comfort in God's pledge to protect the world from another act of total destruction like the flood:**

  Genesis 8 v 22
  As long as the earth endures,
  seedtime and harvest,
  cold and heat,
  summer and winter,
  day and night
  will never cease.

The opening line of that quotation is sometimes understood as a dark hint that the world won't endure forever. But that way of looking at it would rob the verse of the relief it's supposed to bring. What's more, God has only just said: "*Never again* will I curse the ground … and *never again* will I destroy all living creatures" (Genesis 8 v 21). This part of the covenant is God's guarantee to preserve the world for ever. The quotation above simply adds an extra layer of reassurance to verse 21: not only will the earth endure but also the seasons and cycles necessary for human life.

This is confirmed in the New Testament, where the terrifying descriptions of "the day of the Lord" stop short of predicting the world's obliteration. On that day it's unbelievers who will experience "destruction" (2 Peter 3 v 7), while the world will be "laid bare" (v 10).[42] When Jesus compares the day of his return to the flood, he likewise has in mind the taking away of unbelievers, not the world's destruction (Matthew 24 v 39). The consistent teaching of the Bible is that this world is the eternal home of the righteous, while the wicked will be swept away (see for example Psalm 37 v 27-29; 119 v 119; Proverbs 2 v 21-22; 10 v 30; Daniel 2 v 35, 44-45; Zephaniah 3 v 11-12; Matthew 5 v 5; Romans 4 v 13; 8 v 19-21; Hebrews 11 v 8, 13; and Revelation 5 v 10). This strongly implies that the "new earth" we're told about in Revelation 21 v 1 will be the same world that we're currently living in. Its newness will be like the wonderful newness of an expertly renovated house. So although it's right to be concerned about environmental damage, we shouldn't panic when hearing reports of threats to the planet's survival. The world is in God's hands, and he has promised to preserve it as the eternal dwelling place of his people.

- Sometimes the local church we belong to can seem tiny and very insignificant next to the great crowds of people all around us who take no interest in Jesus. **We mustn't lose confidence in God because of the relatively small number of his people.** At one point the entire population of the world was punished with just eight people saved. The pattern throughout salvation history has been for a small remnant to be saved, while a much larger number of people reject God. It's true that Jesus encourages us to expect a great harvest from the preaching of the gospel (Matthew 9 v 37-38). But he also teaches that believers will always be in the minority: "Wide is the gate and broad is the road that leads to destruction, and many enter through it. But small is the gate and narrow the road that leads to life, and only a few find it" (Matthew 7 v 13-14). It's only when God's people are gathered together in the New Jerusalem that we'll form a multitude too great to count (Revelation 7 v 9).

Chapter 6

The Covenant with Abraham

"To your descendants I give this land"

Genesis 15 v 18

The story so far

Adam and Eve broke the covenant made with God in the Garden of Eden. They rejected God and his good rule, choosing Satan's influence instead. But God gave them a way to escape the punishment they deserved through another covenant, which spoke of the future defeat of Satan by one of their own descendants. Tragically, however, mankind echoed the original rebellion in the garden, turning away from God once again. He decided to destroy humanity, but he rescued Noah and his family from the flood. Through a third covenant, God guaranteed the preservation of the world.

Introducing the covenant with Abraham

Each of the covenants we've looked at so far has been presented at a time of new beginnings for God's people. The same is true of the covenant with Abraham. On this occasion salvation history needs rebooting because of the building of the Tower of Babel. At first glance the tower might seem like a harmless architectural experiment but in fact it's mankind's declaration of war against God:

Genesis 11 v 4-8, ESV

Then they said, "Come, let us build ourselves a city and a tower with its top in the heavens, and let us make a name for ourselves, lest we be dispersed over the face of the whole earth." And the LORD came down to see the city and the tower, which the children of man had built. And the LORD said, "Behold, they are one people, and they have all one language, and this is only the beginning of what they will do. And nothing that they propose to do will now be impossible for them. Come, let us go down and there confuse their language, so that they may not understand one another's speech." So the LORD dispersed them from there over the face of all the earth, and they left off building the city.

Three things in this passage reveal man's hostility to God. First, instead of seeking to glorify the LORD, the people openly admit their desire to "make a name" for themselves. Second, they say they want to exalt themselves "lest we be dispersed over the face of the whole earth." In other words, the tower is a muscle-flexing exercise designed to intimidate God and put him off the idea of interfering with them. Third, in refusing to be scattered throughout the earth they're rejecting God's creational decree to "fill the earth and subdue it" (Genesis 1 v 28).

So the Tower of Babel is a smoking gun: indisputable evidence of a world desperate to be rid of its Creator – his reputation, his presence and his commands. After the rebellion in Eden and the worldwide rejection of God before the flood, it's increasingly clear that human history is stuck on repeat.

But it's always impossible for mankind to win a victory over the Creator. "There is no wisdom, no insight, no plan that can succeed against the LORD" (Proverbs 21 v 30). With one brilliant strike – the confusing of man's language – God triumphs over the insurgents on all three fronts. His name is glorified; their attempt to look intimidating ends up making them a laughing stock (see Luke 14 v 28-30); and the scattering that humanity tried to avoid is brought about (see Genesis 10 v 5, 20, 31-32).

Babel means "confused", which accurately describes the situation as the labourers and bricklayers working on the tower suddenly can't understand one another. It's like the "formless" state of the universe before the first day of creation week (Genesis 1 v 2). Salvation history needs to regain traction and that happens when a child is born to a barren couple called Abraham and Sarah. Reflecting on this, Paul says that God "calls into existence the things that do not exist" (Romans 4 v 17, ESV). That language puts the birth of Abraham's child on a par with the creation of the world itself. What's more, Abraham is described by Paul as "the father of us all" (Romans 4 v 16), a remarkable claim to make about one human being, post-Adam. This is a re-start of creational proportions, and so, as we should expect, it's the backdrop for another covenant.

The covenant with Abraham is spread over several chapters in Genesis. The main contents of the covenant are found in 12 v 1-7, the covenant ceremony takes place in chapter 15, and the commitment expected of Abraham is set out in 17 v 1-22.

Covenant contents
In Genesis chapter 12 God tells Abraham that he'll be the father of a nation, based not in Abraham's hometown of Ur but a thousand miles west, in Canaan. So there are two key elements to God's covenant offer: descendants and land.

1. Descendants

We've already seen how important it is to have descendants in Old Testament times. God's people need children to be successful in their job of cultivating the world. On top of that, humanity's only hope is an as-yet-unborn saviour. So after many years of childlessness Abraham must be overjoyed about this part of God's promise. Later on he's told that his offspring will be as numerous as the stars. God changes his name from the original Abram, meaning "my father is exalted", to Abraham, which loosely translated means "Mr Family Tree".

By the end of Genesis, Abraham's descendants have become a nation known as Israel (Genesis 49 v 16, 28). The rest of the Bible is obsessed with the fortunes of this one nation. Even a vast superpower like the Roman Empire barely gets a mention in the Bible, but Israel never leaves its pages, all the way to the end (see Revelation 21 v 12). That shouldn't surprise us in view of Genesis 12 v 3, which says that Abraham's nation will bless the whole world. At this point we need to put two and two together. We've already seen that the promised saviour is the world's sole hope, and now we find that Israel will bring God's blessing to the world. That can only mean that mankind's champion is going to be an Israelite.

In fact God is so focused on the presence of the saviour among Abraham's descendants that it's as if he's Abraham's only offspring. Paul says: "The promises were spoken to Abraham and to his seed. The Scripture does not say 'and to seeds', meaning many people, but 'and to your seed', meaning one person, who is Christ" (Galatians 3 v 16). Traditional wooden "Matryoshka" dolls from Russia fit inside one another, with the complete set nestling inside the largest doll. You can think of the set as many dolls or just one doll (containing all the others). When God thinks of Abraham's offspring, he sees them as contained within just one descendant – the promised saviour.

This Russian doll principle is very important. We can tell from Paul's letter to the Galatians that the first Gentile believers in Jesus felt somewhat inferior to the Israelite believers, as if they were second-class citizens. They were unsure whether they really stood to inherit the promises made to Abraham and his offspring. Paul reassures them by explaining that, spiritually speaking, they *are* Abraham's descendants: "If you belong to Christ, then you are Abraham's seed, and heirs according to the promise" (Galatians 3 v 29). They're like the smaller dolls safely stowed inside the mother doll (Christ), and so through the mother doll's membership of Israel they too are citizens of "the Israel of God" (Galatians 6 v 16), included in "the circumcision" (Philippians 3 v 3), and members of "the twelve tribes" (James 1 v 1). By the same token, Abraham's physical descendants aren't automatically full members of Abraham's nation or "true Israelites" (see John 1 v 47). In Jesus' words, Abraham's "descendants" aren't necessarily his "children" (see John 8 v 37, 39).

But we shouldn't get the idea that physical descent from Abraham is insignificant or irrelevant. Although no one ever truly belongs to God's covenant people without keeping his covenant (see Psalm 103 v 17-18), there's still a sense in which Abraham's physical descendants were and are God's covenant people. That's the clear implication of God's instruction to Abraham concerning circumcision in Genesis 17 v 13: "My covenant in your flesh is to be an everlasting covenant." 2 Chronicles 6 v 11 speaks of "the covenant of the LORD that he made with the people of Israel." Paul says of unbelieving Israelites: "Theirs is the adoption as sons;

theirs the divine glory, the covenants" (Romans 9 v 4); and "God's gifts and his call are irrevocable" (Romans 11 v 29).

This doesn't mean that all Jewish people receive all the benefits of covenant relationship with God – as we've just seen, full membership of Israel is reserved for those who belong to Israel's saviour. But it does mean that those blessings are made available to them in a special way (see Romans 1 v 16 and Acts 13 v 46), and that God has a special longing for them to receive those benefits, because "they are loved on account of the patriarchs" (Romans 11 v 28). With great privilege comes great responsibility: Paul says that on "the day of God's wrath, when his righteous judgment will be revealed … there will be trouble and distress for every human being who does evil: first for the Jew, then for the Gentile" (Romans 2 v 5, 9). The great Scottish preacher, Robert Murray M'Cheyne, draws out the significance of Paul's warning:

> *It is an awful thought that the Jew will be the first to stand forward at the bar of God to be judged … When the Son of Man shall come in His glory, and all the holy angels with Him … when the awful sentence comes forth from His lips, depart ye cursed – and when the guilty many shall move away from before Him into everlasting punishment – is it not enough to make the most careless among you pause and consider, that the indignation and wrath shall first come upon the Jew – that their faces will gather deeper paleness, their knees knock more against each other, and their hearts die within them more than others?[43]*

2. Land

Speak to anyone who's just bought a house, and you'll find out the importance of land. It may be only a smallish rectangle of soil but it's large enough to have a house on it, which makes that patch of ground very precious to its owners. We love to have our own living space, and this longing would have been even greater in ancient times when people used their own land to grow food. No doubt Abraham's heart rejoices at the LORD's words: "To your offspring I will give this land" (Genesis 12 v 7). A later passage makes it clear that Abraham himself is included in the promise: "The LORD said to Abram after Lot had parted from him, 'Lift up your eyes from where you are and look north and south, east and west. All the land that you see I will give to you and your offspring for ever'" (13 v 14-15).

The problem facing anyone who reads to the end of the Abraham narratives in Genesis is that he never gets the land. As Stephen puts it in Acts chapter 7: "[God] gave him no inheritance here, not even a foot of ground" (verse 5). It looks as if God wasn't true to his word, but that's impossible because God never lies (Titus 1 v 2). So in what sense does Abraham receive the promised land? The book of Hebrews gives us the answer:

Hebrews 11 v 8-16

By faith Abraham ... made his home in the promised land like a stranger in a foreign country; he lived in tents, as did Isaac and Jacob, who were heirs with him of the same promise ... All these people were still living by faith when they died. They did not receive the things promised; they only saw them and welcomed them from a distance. And they admitted that they were aliens and strangers on earth. People who say such things show that they are looking for a country of their own ... they were longing for a better country – a heavenly one. Therefore God is not ashamed to be called their God, for he has prepared a city for them.

In other words, Abraham knew perfectly well that he would not receive the land in this life. Like other Old Testament saints, he believed in life beyond the grave (see for example Genesis 49 v 18, 33; Job 19 v 23-27; Psalm 16 v 10-11; Proverbs 11 v 19; 12 v 28; Daniel 12 v 2, 13). Abraham trusted that after his death he would receive the land promised by God in the covenant.

The land in question stretches from the Mediterranean Sea to the River Euphrates (Genesis 15 v 18). And just like the nation of Israel, it stays in the Bible's spotlight from this point onwards. For about a thousand years of Bible history, between the escape from Egypt and the Babylonian conquest, at least part of it belongs to the people of Israel. But when we read about Israel losing ownership of the land, we shouldn't be overly concerned, because it will belong to Abraham and his offspring in the end. The covenant guarantees that.[44]

Covenant ceremony

Let's hope Abraham wasn't squeamish at the sight of internal organs. Under instruction from God, he has to split several animals into two and arrange the halves opposite each other (Genesis 15 v 10). He's then greeted by one of the Bible's strangest scenes:

Genesis 15 v 17-18

When the sun had set and darkness had fallen, a smoking brazier with a blazing torch appeared and passed between the pieces. On that day the LORD made a covenant with Abram and said, "To your descendants I give this land".

A brazier (a sort of portable oven) and a torch (a pole with flaming rags tied at the top) are hovering in mid-air. No doubt Abraham rubs his eyes and pinches himself as he looks at such astonishing things. The brazier and the torch then pass between the severed animals.

The meaning of this extraordinary event is not hard to grasp. The smoking brazier and the flaming torch are symbols of God's presence (see Exodus 13 v 21). By passing through the torn animal pieces, God is making the covenant pledge: "I face death if I fail to keep the terms of this covenant." At this point we're expecting Abraham to pass through the carcasses too – that's the norm for covenant ceremonies.

But he doesn't.

We can only draw one conclusion from this twist to the usual procedure: God will pay the price for covenant failure by either side. Now, it's impossible for God to dishonour the covenant – because he always keeps his promises – but it's highly likely that Abraham will fail to keep his side of the agreement. So God is saying that he's willing to die on behalf of Abraham and his descendants. If they fall short of the covenant's terms, he'll take the curse for covenant failure in their place. This explains why God credits Abraham with righteousness the moment he says "yes" to the covenant offer (Genesis 15 v 6). The ceremony of the smoking oven and burning torch is therefore a foreshadowing of the cross of Jesus. As O. Palmer Robertson comments, "In Jesus Christ God fulfils his promise. In him God is with us. He offers his own body and his own blood as victim of the covenantal curses. His flesh is torn that God's word to [Abraham] might be fulfilled."[45]

Covenant commitment

Covenants always impose obligations on both sides. God's willingness to take the punishment in Abraham's place underlines that principle, because if Abraham had no covenantal obligations, he wouldn't incur the covenant curse – so there would be no punishment for God to receive. Abraham's obligations under the covenant are found in Genesis chapter 17. He needs to be committed to blamelessness and to undergo circumcision.

1. Blamelessness

> **Genesis 17 v 1**
> When Abram was ninety-nine years old, the Lord appeared to him and said, "I am God Almighty; walk before me and be blameless."

What an impossible command! How could anyone be blameless in the sight of such a good, pure and holy God? We might expect Abraham to give up immediately and set off back to Ur, shaking his head in frustration. But we need to bear in mind the message of the covenant ceremony in chapter 15. God knows very well that Abraham won't achieve perfect blamelessness. That's why he himself goes through the animal pieces in Abraham's place.

What God seeks through this command is an ongoing commitment from Abraham to aim for blamelessness day by day. Of course he'll swerve from the path and act in blameworthy ways (see for example Genesis chapter 20). But he must then get back on track – even when a certain act of obedience might be the last thing he wants to do (see chapter 22). Aiming for blamelessness is part of the covenant.

To illustrate this, imagine two ships in the early nineteenth century. One belongs to the Royal Navy, the other flies the skull and crossbones. The pirate ship is in conflict with the Navy ship and would gladly destroy it if given the opportunity. The pirates laugh scornfully at the idea of taking orders from the Royal Navy captain. In contrast, the sailors on board the Navy vessel love their captain and desire to serve him blamelessly.

The problem is, they constantly let him down. At the end of each day they have to admit they've patched up sails shabbily, scrubbed decks half-heartedly, and generally failed to serve their captain in a blameless way. But ask any of those Navy sailors if they're serious about pleasing the captain and they'll confirm that they genuinely do want to be faultless in his service. There's clearly a world of difference between the pirates and the Navy sailors. They don't share the same attitude towards the Navy captain and his orders. Abraham needs to have that Navy-style commitment to the LORD and his commands. If he takes after the pirates by scorning God's ways, he'll be rejecting the covenant and will no longer receive its blessings.[46]

2. Circumcision

Genesis 17 v 10-12, 14

Every male among you shall be circumcised. You are to undergo circumcision, and it will be the sign of the covenant between me and you. For the generations to come every male among you who is eight days old must be circumcised ... Any uncircumcised male, who has not been circumcised in the flesh, will be cut off from his people; he has broken my covenant.

God says that circumcision is the "sign of the covenant". Just as the rainbow was the emblem of the covenant with Noah, so circumcision represents the covenant with Abraham. God has just told Abraham to remove what is blameworthy from his life. Now he's telling him to cut off an unclean piece of his body.[47] The symbolic connection is obvious. Circumcision is therefore a visual reminder for Abraham of his obligation to get rid of rebelliousness, the foreskin of the heart (see Deuteronomy 10 v 16, ESV). It's fitting that the severed piece of flesh comes from the very body part that will bring the new nation into being. God's gift of descendants is linked to Abraham's willingness to be ruthless with sin.

The bloodiness of circumcision suggests that it's a covenant ceremony, supplementing the ceremony of Genesis 15 v 9-21. As Michael Horton says: "In Genesis 17, the covenant with Abraham and his seed was 'cut' quite literally by the rite of circumcision."[48] Covenant ceremonies threaten the participants with death. Through this ceremony God signifies that Abraham will face death if he rejects the covenant. God's pledge to receive the covenant curse himself, witnessed by Abraham in the earlier ceremony, does not apply to those who defiantly reject covenant relationship with him. As verse 14 says: "Any uncircumcised male ... will be cut off from his people; he has broken my covenant."

Moses and Jeremiah later cry out to the Israelites: "Circumcise your hearts" (Deuteronomy 10 v 16; Jeremiah 4 v 4). The Israelites in those days were outwardly circumcised, but inwardly rebellious. They were like a man cheating on his wife who feels sure his marriage is going well simply because he still wears his wedding ring. But the ring, of course, is just a symbol of his commitment to his wife, and means nothing if he doesn't acknowledge that commitment in his heart. Moses and Jeremiah are warning Israel that physical circumcision isn't the only covenant obligation that needs to be taken seriously. Further on in the Bible,

Paul says that circumcision of the heart is something that can only be carried out "by the Spirit" (Romans 2 v 29). By nature, no fallen human being is truly ruthless with sin, but with God's help sin can be fought and progress can be made towards blamelessness.

In new covenant times outward circumcision ceases to be compulsory for God's people (Galatians 5 v 6; although in the case of Timothy it served a useful evangelistic purpose – see Acts 16 v 1-3). The foreskin is therefore included in the large category of things that are declared clean. But the other clauses of the covenant with Abraham endure throughout salvation history.

Life lessons

- **The covenant with Abraham teaches us that if we trust in Jesus, we've joined a nation, the "Israel of God"** (Galatians 6 v 16). It's as if we each have a spiritual passport saying *Israel* on the front.[49] Everyone who belongs to this nation should matter to us deeply. It can be difficult to love believers from a different culture, or from a church that does things very differently to our own. But we need to remember that we're all like wooden dolls nestling inside one single doll – Jesus, our saviour. He gives our nation its identity and unity, and we need to treat our fellow-citizens well for his sake. The Israel of God will be strong when we stop treating other believers like unwanted strangers; when we no longer let minor differences flare up into major disputes; and when believing churches stop acting like isolated islands and begin working together with other gospel-preaching churches in their area. We should live out the national unity that is ours through Jesus. When we love one another, find common ground with one another, and work in partnership with one another, the Israel of God will flourish.

- **Through the covenant with Abraham, believers have also joined a new family.** Zacchaeus, for example, is called "a son of Abraham" when he turns from a life of extortion to follow Jesus (Luke 19 v 9). A disabled woman who responds to Jesus' invitation is called "a daughter of Abraham" (Luke 13 v 16). They share the all-important family likeness: not hair colour, or dimples in their cheeks, but faith in the covenant promises of God. It's so encouraging that Jesus describes believers as sons of Abraham or daughters of Abraham, because you can't stop being someone's son. You never stop being someone's daughter. Being a son or daughter of Abraham is something that lasts throughout all eternity.

- Abraham is told to circumcise his son on the eighth day after his birth (Genesis 17 v 12). This shows that **God wants children to be raised within the covenant community**. Later on they may choose to reject God and his eternal covenant. But unless and until that time arrives, they're to be treated as full members of God's covenant people. God says: "You must keep my covenant, you and your descendants after you for the generations to come" (17 v 9); and "This is my covenant with you and your descendants after you" (17 v 10). The Bible never agrees with the view that children should be left alone to believe whatever they want to believe. In new covenant times, Paul calls on fathers to raise their children "in the discipline and instruction of the Lord" (Ephesians 6 v 4, ESV).

- **Blamelessness means living without fault in God's service.** Pursuing it is part of the eternal covenant (Psalm 119 v 1; Philippians 1 v 10). We're certainly not saved *by* blameless service, but we are saved *for* blameless service. Jesus urges: "Be perfect ... as your heavenly Father is perfect" (Matthew 5 v 48). As the *ESV Study Bible* comments: "The perfection of the Father ... is what all Jesus' disciples are called to pursue." Are you conscious of letting Jesus down in a certain way? Is there something you could do to change that? Why not renew your personal commitment to blamelessness today? All over the world believers are picking themselves up, dusting themselves down and getting back on the path of obedience. As Dale Ralph Davis has written: "The Christian life is a life of continual repentance, ever in need of renewing its allegiance to the rule of Yahweh."[50] If we've grown tired of repenting and are clinging to a certain sin, we should ask ourselves which ship we want to belong to: the rebel ship, or the covenant ship?

Perhaps we need to remind ourselves of the Bible's warnings for those who stop aiming for blamelessness: "If I had cherished sin in my heart, the LORD would not have listened" (Psalm 66 v 18). *Do you really want God to refuse to listen to you?* "For if you live according to the sinful nature, you will die" (Romans 8 v 13). *Do you really want to turn your back on eternal life?* Stay on the covenant ship, the ship that grants full forgiveness to its crew. Aim unswervingly for blamelessness, "with the strength God provides" (1 Peter 4 v 11).

- **We shouldn't feel embarrassed to look forward to the day when we will "inherit the earth"** (Matthew 5 v 5). Abraham and his spiritual children will receive the land of Israel, along with all the other countries, territories and islands of this world. We won't be perched on clouds in luminous nightgowns, plucking the ten-stringed lyre. No, our future dwelling place is land. It's "a new heaven and a new *earth*" (Revelation 21 v 1). Perhaps your current living space is a small rented room in a run-down shared house. There's not nearly enough storage space in the kitchen. The bathroom makes you shudder, and it's debatable whether using it will make you cleaner or more germy. You long to have better land. Perhaps God will bless you with boundary lines in pleasanter places in this world (Psalm 16 v 6). But whether or not that happens, the covenant with Abraham encourages us to look forward to better real estate in the world to come – surpassing the finest English country house, or the grandest French chateau, or the roomiest Texan ranch. There are other, deeper reasons to long for Jesus' return, but that doesn't mean we should overlook the promise of land. It's a powerful reminder that we do not need to store up treasures in this world, "where thieves break in and steal" (Matthew 6 v 19). Better things are coming.

Chapter 7

The Covenant with Moses:

"The Ten Commandments" Deuteronomy 4 v 13

The story so far

A covenant binds two parties together, on the basis of agreed terms. In the Garden of Eden the first humans violated the original covenant with God. They faced the covenant punishment of death. But through a second covenant God graciously promised a saviour. This was also rejected by all but a few. In response God sent a flood to destroy the earth, but he saved Noah and his family, and through a further covenant he pledged to preserve the world. Then rebellion flared up again at Babel. Abraham and Sarah – an old man and his barren wife – were called by God to a distant country. God promised Abraham that he and his descendants would inherit the land.

Introducing the covenant with Moses

The descendants of Abraham, by now "exceedingly numerous" (Exodus 1 v 7), are living as slaves in Egypt. But God takes action to give them a fresh start. They leave the spiritual darkness of pagan Egypt and travel to "a good and spacious land" (Exodus 3 v 8). On the way they experience a rescue just like Noah's escape from the flood:

Exodus 15 v 19

When Pharaoh's horses, chariots and horsemen went into the sea, the LORD brought the waters of the sea back over them, but the Israelites walked through the sea on dry ground.

The land of milk and honey awaits them. At this foundational time God makes another covenant with his people. The Israelites need instructions for building their nation state, which explains why law is the signature feature of the covenant with Moses.

The grace that comes before the law

If ever someone has saviour credentials, it's Moses. Even at birth he stands out as "a fine child" (Exodus 2 v 2), or as the New Testament puts it, "no ordinary child" (Hebrews 11 v 23). But he's born at a time when a new Pharaoh has ruled that every male Israelite baby must be drowned in the Nile. When it becomes impossible for Moses' mother to keep him hidden, she lays him in a basket made from papyrus reeds. The Hebrew word translated "basket" is the same word that the Bible uses for Noah's ark. What's more, Moses' mother coats the basket with pitch (Exodus 2 v 3), just like the ark (Genesis 6 v 14). It looks as if she's copying one of her people's salvation stories in the hope of rescuing her son.

His paper ark drifts towards some young girls bathing in the river, a group from the royal court including Pharaoh's daughter. The baby wins her heart and she decides to raise him as her son. But in the meantime he's handed back to his own mother to be nursed, after his sister – who's kept an eye on proceedings from the riverbank – suggests it might be good for an Israelite woman to nurse the boy. So Moses' mother gets to care for her baby in peace, and has the added bonus of wages paid by the palace (Exodus 2 v 9). It's a sensational tale of deliverance.

Not only does Moses have this back-story of personal salvation, he also has the advantage of the best upbringing available in Egypt. As the son of Pharaoh's daughter, he's "educated in all the wisdom of the Egyptians", and he grows up to be "powerful in speech and action" (Acts 7 v 22). But despite all this, he still remembers his origins and considers the Israelites "his own people" (Exodus 2 v 11). He wants to rescue them from their suffering, and so he's willing to step in to defend them (Acts 7 v 24). Everything about this man suggests that he will save his people.

Then it all falls apart. The Bible says: "Moses thought that his own people would realise that God was using him to rescue them, but they did not" (Acts 7 v 25). He's forced to flee the country. He marries the daughter of a pagan priest and settles in the land of Midian, far from Egypt and the Israelites. The only people he successfully rescues are some Midianite girls from a group of aggressive shepherds (Exodus 2 v 17). It's a gentlemanly act but it's hardly the rescue everyone has been hoping for. His own people remain in slavery far away, toiling for their cruel masters. Moses himself admits that his ambition to save the Israelites has ended in total failure. As he puts down further roots in Midian with the birth of his first child, he declares: "I have become an alien in a foreign land" (Exodus 2 v 22).

Moses' lack of success, despite all his qualifications, shows who the real saviour is. Just when the rescue graph has reached its lowest point, there's an upward tick:

Exodus 2 v 23-25

During that long period, the king of Egypt died. The Israelites groaned in their slavery and cried out, and their cry for help because of their slavery went up to God. God heard their groaning and he remembered his covenant with Abraham, with Isaac and with Jacob. So God looked on the Israelites and was concerned about them.

The message is clear: salvation belongs to God. Although he goes on to use Moses as his instrument, it would be a serious mistake to focus on the part Moses plays. It's the grace of God, rather than Israel's own strength, which brings about the new beginning away from Egypt's slave drivers. Moses himself makes exactly that point:

Deuteronomy 4 v 37
Because he loved your forefathers and chose their descendants after them, he brought you out of Egypt by his Presence and his great strength.

From first to last, the rescue from Egypt is down to God. It's achieved by his strength, and motivated by his love.[51]

It's important for us to see this before we look at the law itself. The law can be demoralising. It doesn't take long to see how far short of it we fall. We begin to wonder if God really wants to have anything to do with sinners like us. We need to remember that the Israelites were redeemed from Egypt before the law was given at Sinai. The order of their salvation is clear: redemption comes before law keeping. God underscores this point just before setting out the terms of the covenant with Moses. In the verse that precedes the Ten Commandments he says: "I am the LORD your God, who brought you out of Egypt, out of the land of slavery" (Exodus 20 v 2). God rescues his people from slavery before they have heard and obeyed his law.

The goodness that comes with the law

In 1531 Sir Thomas Elyot declared: "In football there is nothing but beastly fury and extreme violence, whereof proceedeth hurt, and consequently rancour and malice do remain with them that be wounded."[52] Yet nowadays football (soccer) is known as "the beautiful game". It has spread from Britain throughout the world, and is played everywhere from vast stadiums to dusty backstreets. The game's beauty and its phenomenal popularity were brought about by one thing: law.

In 1848 a group of students at Cambridge University drew up the rules that brought modern football into being. Twenty-five years later the first international match was played, after a further twenty-five years football was included in the Olympic Games, and thirty years later the first World Cup was staged in Uruguay – on the other side of the world from Cambridge. All this resulted from the healthy influence of law.

The writers of the Bible wouldn't be at all surprised by the beneficial impact of rules on football. They're all pro-law. The writer of Psalm 119 is particularly enthusiastic. The theme of his 176-verse psalm is the wonder of God's law. He describes it as "sweeter than honey" (verse 103), "the joy of my heart" (verse 111), "a light for my path" (verse 105), and "more precious to me than thousands of pieces of silver and gold" (verse 72). He goes so far as to say, "My soul is consumed with longing for your laws at all times" (verse 20), and, "I open my mouth and pant, longing for your commands" (verse 131).

One thing he says about God's law seems especially countercultural today: "I will walk about in freedom, for I have sought out your precepts" (verse 45). Compare that with the Rolling Stones' line: "I'm free to do what I want, any old time." For the Stones, freedom comes with lawlessness, and that way of thinking didn't die out in the Sixties. But the Rolling Stones are wrong. Doing "what I want" means saying "yes" to sinful temptations. Sin traps people (Proverbs 22 v 5); it draws people into deep pits (Proverbs 23 v 27); it chains people up in slavery (John 8 v 34). That's not freedom! We need God's law to help us avoid sin, and then – as the psalm-writer says – we can walk about freely.

The covenant with Moses moves salvation history forward in the area of law. It puts flesh on the bones of that short command in the covenant with Abraham: "Be blameless" (Genesis 17 v 1). Law is so prominent in this covenant that sometimes the phrase "the Ten Commandments" is used interchangeably with "the covenant" (see for example Exodus 34 v 28). It's important to see this as a positive development in salvation history.[53] Each covenant adds good things to the overarching eternal covenant, and as we've just seen, law is immensely valuable. As O. Palmer Robertson says, the covenant with Moses brings about "a new stage in the ... unfolding richness of the covenant of redemption."[54]

The guilt that comes from the law

On the morning of the giving of the Ten Commandments, the Israelites wake to the sound of thunder (Exodus 19 v 16). This is no distant rumble, it's detonating overhead. As the Israelites roll back their tent flaps to investigate, they see lighting bolts repeatedly striking the summit of Mount Sinai, which is covered by thick cloud. Then a strange and unnerving sound comes from the top of the mountain. Perfectly distinct through the thunder, there's a long and very loud blast of the *shofar* – a trumpet made from a ram's horn. How could any *shofar* be big enough to make such a sound? And who could be blowing on it? Parents gather their children close to them as they draw near to the mountain. Then everyone shrinks back at an extraordinary sight: fire falls on the mountain as if it's been poured out from a bucket in the sky. The blaze sends up a huge column of smoke. The whole mountain then shakes violently, and the blowing of the *shofar*, which everyone has assumed is at top volume, grows even louder and still louder. Then – above the thunder, and the earthquake, and the trumpet's blasting – there's another sound that's audible to everyone. The Israelites hear the voice of God, declaring his perfect laws in their own Hebrew language (20 v 22, see also Deuteronomy 5 v 22-27). No wonder Scripture says: "They trembled with fear" (Exodus 20 v 18).

Why does God frighten the Israelites? The Bible gives a straight answer to that question: "So that the fear of God will be with you to keep you from sinning" (Exodus 20 v 20). It's not wrong to frighten people to press home a desperately important message. A child on a scooter in the road needs to be yelled at fiercely if a truck is coming. If the Israelites reject God's covenant, they'll receive something far worse than fear alone.

At this point we need to remember the difference between covenant failure and covenant rejection. Those Israelites who sincerely take part in the covenant, striving for blameless obedience, will fall short of its terms. But they're in a completely different category to the Israelites who reject covenant relationship with God. So there are two kinds of listener among the Israelites: covenant believers and covenant rejecters. *Both* will fail to keep the Ten Commandments. But God is well aware of that and so he provides the sacrificial system to assure believers that a substitute's death will atone for their sin. Covenant rejecters can't take any comfort from the sacrificial system because, like the people of Noah's day, or the builders of the Tower of Babel, they're living in sustained rebellion against God. They've turned down his offer of relationship in favour of hardened sinfulness. So the believing Israelites are worlds apart from the covenant rejecters, even though neither group keeps the law perfectly.

In each case the law has a different effect. It shames covenant believers into admitting their many shortcomings. Covenant rejecters, on the other hand, either ignore the law, or refuse to admit their guilt. The latter kind of covenant rejecter can be hard to spot, because on the surface they seem deeply committed to God. One of Jesus' parables gives us a case study. It features a covenant believer and a covenant rejecter from the hard-to-spot group:

Luke 18 v 10-14

Two men went up to the temple to pray, one a Pharisee and the other a tax collector. The Pharisee stood up and prayed about himself: "God, I thank you that I am not like other men – robbers, evildoers, adulterers – or even like this tax collector. I fast twice a week and give a tenth of all I get."

But the tax collector stood at a distance. He would not even look up to heaven, but beat his breast and said, "God, have mercy on me, a sinner."

I tell you that this man, rather than the other, went home justified before God.

The Pharisee won't accept that the law leaves him guilty in God's sight. He doesn't seek mercy from God because he doesn't think he needs mercy. When he reads the law, he ticks every box, not realising that even our righteous acts are like filthy rags (Isaiah 64 v 6). It's a different story with the tax collector. He's overwhelmed by conviction of guilt before a holy God, and so he pleads for mercy in the temple – the site of covenant mercy. The end of the parable shows that the tax collector is truly taking part in the covenant, while the Pharisee is a covenant rejecter despite all his religiosity. His pompous refusal to beg for mercy counts as rebellion because "God opposes the proud" (James 4 v 6). So maybe we should add a third ship to the illustration used in the previous chapter. As well as the covenant ship, and the pirate ship packed with out-and-out rebels, there's a ship staffed by people who think they're serving the covenant captain. But they won't listen to him properly. They won't let his word search their hearts. They won't call out for his mercy and so he cannot have anything to do with them. They're not on his ship.

God's programme to plant holy fear in the Israelites continues with the covenant ceremony set out in Exodus chapter 24. During the ceremony the people are spattered with blood. It reminds them that the rightful penalty for any kind of covenant failure is death:

Exodus 24 v 7-8
Then [Moses] took the Book of the Covenant and read it to the people. They responded, "We will do everything the LORD has said; we will obey." Moses then took the blood, sprinkled it on the people and said, "This is the blood of the covenant that the LORD has made with you in accordance with all these words."

The ceremony is designed to get believers thinking along the following lines: "I've just committed myself to obeying everything God has said. Moses has sprinkled blood on my face and clothes to show that failure to obey deserves death. I sincerely intend to pursue blameless obedience. But I know that I'll fall short of what God requires. How can I possibly be saved?" In this way the guilt stirred up by the law leads covenant believers straight to the sacrificial system and the ultimate sacrifice it points to. As Paul says: "Through the law we become conscious of sin" (Romans 3 v 20).

The glory that comes through the law

Many people setting out to read the whole Bible from start to finish have a similar experience. Genesis and the first half of Exodus keep them gripped. But on reaching Exodus chapter 25 they struggle to stay attentive. That chapter and the six which follow go into seemingly endless detail about anointing oil, scarlet yarn, acacia wood, rams' skins, overlaid frames and bronze tent pegs. The episode of the golden calf in chapters 32 to 34 quickens the reader's pulse again, but then there are six more chapters of clasps, crossbars and finely twisted linen! Why does the Bible take such extreme interest in God's tent, the "tabernacle" or "Tent of Meeting"?

In the garden of Eden Adam and Eve's lives were enriched to an unimaginable degree by the presence of God himself, walking with them (Genesis 3 v 8). Because of the fall that most precious gift was taken away. But now, in the covenant with Moses, a wonderful sentence comes from God's lips:

Exodus 25 v 8
Have them make a sanctuary for me, and I will dwell among them.

The cascade of tabernacle information suddenly makes sense. God is coming back to his people! It's right and proper for every detail of his dwelling place to be so carefully and lovingly recorded.

However, this move forward in salvation history hits a roadblock because of the people's disobedience. In the shadow of Mount Sinai, the Israelites break the second of the Ten Commandments. They worship a golden calf as if it were the LORD himself. It's a blatant rejection of the covenant. In response God says: "I will not go with you, because you are a stiff-necked people and I might destroy you on the way" (Exodus 33 v 3). But Moses, who didn't take part in the calf worship, prays for Israel and God revives his plan to dwell among the people (Exodus 33 v 17). At this critical point in the history of redemption, Moses asks God for a special sign. He says to God: "Now show me your glory" (Exodus 33 v 18), and God agrees.

The event takes place in the morning, on the summit of Mount Sinai. God has already told Moses what will happen:

Exodus 33 v 19, 21-23

The LORD said, "I will cause all my goodness to pass in front of you, and I will proclaim my name, the LORD, in your presence … There is a place near me where you may stand on a rock. When my glory passes by, I will put you in a cleft in the rock and cover you with my hand until I have passed by. Then I will remove my hand and you will see my back; but my face must not be seen."

So there will be two elements to the experience: *majestic visuals* (Moses will see the after-effects of God himself as he passes by), and *meaningful verbals* (Moses will hear God proclaim his name).

Exodus 34 v 5-7

Then the LORD came down in the cloud and stood there

with him and proclaimed his name, the LORD. And he passed in front of Moses, proclaiming, "The LORD, the LORD, the compassionate and gracious God, slow to anger, abounding in love and faithfulness, maintaining love to thousands, and forgiving wickedness, rebellion and sin. Yet he does not leave the guilty unpunished; he punishes the children and their children for the sin of the fathers to the third and fourth generation."

Moses sees God's glory and he hears about God's character. God's willingness to live among the Israelites is good news not only because he's visibly glorious but also because he's compassionate, gracious, loving, faithful, forgiving and holy.

What Moses discovers on Mount Sinai is that God's presence is tied to his word. So it's no coincidence that progress in manifestation (God dwelling with his people) comes with progress in revelation (the giving of the law). Once the tabernacle has been constructed, the epicentre of God's presence is a chest called "the ark of the covenant". Inside it are the two stone tablets inscribed with the Ten Commandments. The connection between God's presence and his word is clear. Now that the people have received more of God's instruction, he comes down to live among them:

Exodus 40 v 34-35
Then the cloud covered the Tent of Meeting, and the glory of the LORD filled the tabernacle. Moses could not enter the Tent of Meeting because the cloud had settled upon it, and the glory of the LORD filled the tabernacle.

- The New Testament takes a good-bad-good-good view
  of the Law of Moses. First of all it's *good*, because it's the
  perfect expression of God's will. Paul sounds just like
  the author of Psalm 119 when he says "So then, the law
  is holy, and the commandment is holy, righteous and
  good" (Romans 7 v 12); and "In my inner being I delight
  in God's law" (verse 22). But the law is *bad* for people
  "trying to be justified by law" (Galatians 5 v 4). For
  them it's a "curse" (Galatians 3 v 13), bringing "death"
  (2 Corinthians 3 v 7), because it pushes them deeper and
  deeper into the quicksand of guilt and punishment. But
  for believers the condemning power of the law is *good*
  because it sends us to Jesus for his rescue by alerting
  us to our guilt (Romans 3 v 20). Finally, for those
  saved through Jesus the law is *good* because it teaches
  us how to live (1 Corinthians 9 v 8-10; James 1 v 25).

  **We should therefore take great care when
  reading the New Testament to work out how the
  word "law" is being used at any one time.** There
  are some negative references to the law, in keeping with
  the bad view explained above, because of the popularity
  at that time of the Pharisees' belief that salvation could
  be obtained through legal observance. The apostles
  obviously had to oppose that misreading of the law
  very firmly. They argued that without salvation through
  Jesus, who is "the end [i.e. goal] of the law" (Romans 10
  v 4), the Law of Moses is worthless (Acts 13 v 39; 15 v 10-
  11). But we mustn't let the Pharisees' misinterpretation
  of the covenant with Moses sour our own attitude to
  the law. Elsewhere in the New Testament it's viewed
  very positively, as we've just seen. Rightly understood,

it's still as thrilling now as it was to the author of Psalm 119.

- **As we read the New Testament, it's clear that some parts of the covenant with Moses no longer need to be observed in new covenant times.** For example, the food laws are revoked in Acts 10 v 12-15. But it's also clear that new covenant believers are expected to obey other parts of the law given to Moses. Paul, for instance, quotes from the Ten Commandments without any hesitation (Romans 13 v 9; Ephesians 6 v 1-2). It's sometimes said that we should only obey the commands that are restated in the New Testament. But covenants don't always go to the trouble of restating the enduring parts of the covenants before them.[55] And we know that the first believers in Jesus obeyed all of the law, with the approval of the apostles (see Acts 21 v 20-26). So the ball is in our court: we're obliged to give a biblical reason for any non-observance of the Law of Moses. To do that we'll need to keep in mind three principles that come straight from the New Testament.
  1. **Ceremonial laws no longer apply,** because God's people no longer worship at the temple (see John 4 v 20-23; Hebrews 9 v 9-10).
  2. **Civil laws no longer apply,** because God's people are no longer a single nation state (see Romans 13 v 1; James 1 v 1).
  3. **Cultural laws no longer apply**, because God's people now come from "every nation, tribe, people and language" (Revelation 7 v 9; see also Galatians 2 v 1-3, 14).[56]

That's not to say the ceremonial, civil and cultural laws no longer have anything to teach us. Jesus says:

"I tell you the truth, until heaven and earth disappear, not the smallest letter, not the least stroke of a pen, will by any means disappear from the Law until everything is accomplished" (Matthew 5 v 18). There are many reasons why each part of the law still matters. The food laws, for example, which were given to distinguish Israel from the other nations (Leviticus 20 v 24-26), help us see the importance of distinctive godliness (1 Peter 1 v 14-16; 2 v 9-12).

- **Much of the Law of Moses stands today as God's ongoing moral code.** That's particularly true of the Ten Commandments, which summarise the law. There was a time when every child in every church could have rattled off the Ten Commandments as soon as they were asked. Nowadays it's hard to find an adult church member who can do that. We're the ones in the Dark Ages.

  Perhaps this decline has been caused by confusion over "legalism". Legalism is seeking to earn salvation through obedience. It's a lethal error that we must avoid (Galatians 5 v 4). But if believers, confident that they've been saved, obey God's commands to please him, that's hardly the same thing as legalism! Obedience is part of pleasing God, because of the nature of who he is and who we are. We must remember that we're in covenant relationship with the ruler of the universe. He doesn't make gentle suggestions like an elderly aunt. He doesn't offer well-meaning advice like a next-door neighbour. He issues commands to be obeyed. To reject them is to walk away from the relationship (see John 15 v 10 or Romans 8 v 7).

  One good first step would be to learn the Ten

Commandments by heart, because it's hard to obey them if you're foggy about what they say. If you're not willing to learn them, even in shorthand form, ask yourself what it is in your heart that makes you unwilling. Is it wise to listen to that part of your heart?[57]

- **The covenant with Moses demonstrates the strong connection between God's presence and his word.** This is hugely significant for anyone wanting to draw near to God. The same principle can be observed in the book of Isaiah. After commissioning Isaiah to, "Comfort, comfort my people" (Isaiah 40 v 1), God immediately says, "Speak tenderly to Jerusalem" (verse 2). He throws his arms around his people through Scripture – and he's still doing that today. The Bible is always a good place to go if you want to get closer to God.

- The least accessible area of the tabernacle was the Holy of Holies (also known as the Most Holy Place), which was guarded by a thick internal curtain. It would be hard to imagine tighter entry requirements. Israel's high priest was the only person in the whole world allowed inside, on just one set day each year (see Leviticus chapter 16). This showed that God and mankind were not yet walking together in the way they had in Eden. But there's a breathtaking development in new covenant times. Translated literally, John 1 v 14 says: "The Word became flesh and tabernacled among us". The Son of God came down from heaven to live among sinful people without any barriers. And when he died on the cross as the perfect sacrifice for sin, the curtain in front of the Most Holy Place was ripped in two (Mark

the covenant with David

ts we've looked at so far have each been made
najor commencement in salvation history. The
th David is no exception, as Psalm 78 makes
Canaan has been conquered, the land is divided
the twelve tribes of Israel:

v 55

nations before them
their lands to them as an inheritance;
tribes of Israel in their homes.

s now in place for the people to honour God by
covenant. Sadly, what happens next is all too

56-58

God to the test and rebelled against the Most High;
keep his statutes.
hers they were disloyal and faithless,
as a faulty bow.
him with their high places;
his jealousy with their idols.

overstate the danger of this situation. This
t failure, in the way that Jacob, for example,
t God down while nonetheless holding on to
. This is in-your-face covenant rejection.
onse is uncompromising, because he "cannot
g" (Habakkuk 1 v 13):

59-61

eard them, he was very angry;

15 v 38), providing barrier-free access to God the Father.
But that's not all. Because Jesus has made his people
holy (Hebrews 10 v 10), God now dwells inside us by his
Spirit, so *each one of us is a mini-tabernacle* (1 Corinthians
6 v 19). **That means if you're a believer, you're
never alone.** In Jesus, and through his work, we see
the full extent of God's desire to be with his people. If
Moses fell to his knees in worship (Exodus 34 v 8), how
much more should we?

Chapter 8

The Covena
with David:

"I will establish his thr

The story so far

God gave mankind the role of
He himself walked with Adar
where all their needs were met.
route, breaking the creational
penalty. Then they received une.
back to God through the devil-c
This second covenant was also
the world with a flood, but sa
waters. A third covenant reassu
not be destroyed again, and
Hostilities between earth and h
the Tower of Babel. But God pc
covenant. He promised land to
bless the world. After the relea
Egypt, a fifth covenant told Go
made provision for the tabernac
his people again.

Introducir
The coven
alongside
covenant
clear. After
up betwee

Psalm 7
He drove
and allott
he settled

Everythin
keeping h
familiar:

Psalm
But they
they did
Like thei
as unreli
They an
they aro

It's hard
isn't cov
frequent
the cove
God's
tolerate

Psalm
When

he rejected Israel completely.
He abandoned the tabernacle of Shiloh,
the tent he had set up among men.
He sent the ark of his might into captivity,
his splendour into the hands of the enemy.

More than anything else in the tabernacle, the ark represents God's dwelling place. So when God sends the ark "into captivity" it's a visual sign of his rejection of Israel. It looks as if salvation history might have come to an end. The ark is described in the Bible as the "ark of the LORD's covenant" (1 Kings 8 v 1), so if the ark goes, so does the covenant. Israel descends into a barren darkness – there are no more marriages and the priests serving at the tabernacle are slaughtered:

Psalm 78 v 62-64
He gave his people over to the sword;
he was very angry with his inheritance.
Fire consumed their young men,
and their maidens had no wedding songs;
their priests were put to the sword,
and their widows could not weep.

The ark is taken away by the Philistines, but God sends "tumours", "rats", and "devastation" to each of the places where it is kept (1 Samuel 5 v 1 – 6 v 12). So the Philistines decide to put it on an unmanned cart pulled by two cows, and wait to see what happens. The cart goes in a straight line towards Israel – a remarkable phenomenon because the cows pulling it are untrained, and are leaving their calves behind them. But while this incident shows that the ark's true home is in the land of Israel, it's not yet a reunion of the LORD with his people. When seventy Israelite men in Beth Shemesh take off the ark's cover to look inside, they're swiftly put to death by God (1 Samuel 6 v 19). The ark ends up in a town called Kiriath Jearim. The tabernacle isn't constructed around it, and it plays no part in Israel's worship. It's plain to see that salvation history remains in crisis.

What happens next reveals the unstoppable nature of God's love for his people:

Psalm 78 v 65-72

Then the LORD awoke as from sleep,
as a man wakes from the stupor of wine.
He beat back his enemies;
he put them to everlasting shame.
Then he rejected the tents of Joseph,
he did not choose the tribe of Ephraim;
but he chose the tribe of Judah,
Mount Zion, which he loved.
He built his sanctuary like the heights,
like the earth that he established for ever.
He chose David his servant
and took him from the sheep pens;
from tending the sheep he brought him
to be the shepherd of his people Jacob,
of Israel his inheritance.
And David shepherded them with integrity of heart;
with skilful hands he led them.

In the middle of that passage the psalm-writer compares this merciful renewal with the creation of the earth itself. Under God, David has a pivotal role. He's the one who takes the ark of the covenant from Kiriath Jearim to Jerusalem, so that

Israel can engage in God-approved worship (1 Chronicles 15 v 25 – 16 v 6).[58] Redemption history is in motion again. Unsurprisingly, God introduces another covenant at this point. There are two main elements in the covenant with David. God promises David a never-ending dynasty, and he commissions a temple to replace the tabernacle.

A house for David

The English market town of Marlborough was served by an unbroken line of doctors from the same family for more than two centuries. The dynasty began with Dr Thelwall Maurice, who came to the town in 1792, and it ended with the retirement of his great-great-great grandson Dr David Maurice in 2009. Funnily enough, David Maurice's son James is also a qualified doctor, but he decided against settling in Marlborough despite admitting it had been "quite high on my list of options."[59] It must have given the residents of Marlborough a pleasing sense of stability as generation after generation of Dr Maurices stepped into the boots of their forebears. In the covenant with David, God introduces the same kind of continuity to the kingship of Israel.

In 2 Samuel chapter 7, God tells David that he'll have a house. The Hebrew word translated "house" can mean either a dwelling place or a dynasty. (As it happens, the English word "house" has the same double meaning: while it usually refers to a dwelling place, it can also be used for a family line – the current British royal family is known as "the house of Windsor".) God makes a series of promises about the house of David:

2 Samuel 7 v 11-16

The LORD declares to you that the LORD himself will establish a house for you: when your days are over and you rest with your fathers, I will raise up your offspring to succeed you, who will come from your own body, and I will establish his kingdom. He is the one who will build a house for my Name, and I will establish the throne of his kingdom for ever. I will be his father, and he shall be my son. When he does wrong, I will punish him with the rod of men, with floggings inflicted by men. But my love will never be taken away from him, as I took it away from Saul, whom I removed from before you. Your house and your kingdom shall endure for ever before me; your throne shall be established for ever.

At first it seems that the LORD is talking about just one of David's descendants. But this is another example of the Russian doll principle, where one person is seen as containing a whole group of people. That's how David himself understands God's message, as we can tell from the following summary that he gives to his son Solomon:

1 Kings 2 v 2-4
Observe what the LORD your God requires ... so that you may prosper in all you do and wherever you go, and that the LORD may keep his promise to me: "If your descendants [literally: sons] watch how they live, and if they walk faithfully before me with all their heart and soul, you will never fail to have a man on the throne of Israel."

Note how "son" in the singular has become "sons" in the plural, and "he" has become "they". Through this covenant God is promising David a line of sons who will reign over Israel.

It's important to ask how this covenant clause affects God's salvation plan. To explore that question we need to return to Israel's rebellion before the time of David. Psalm 78 doesn't exaggerate when it says that the tribes of Israel "put God to the test" (verse 56). One particularly dark episode in the book of Judges demonstrates Israel's rebellion. A man goes on a journey with his concubine (concubines were women who acted as wives without the same status and rights as a wife). He decides not to lodge in the pagan city of Jebus, but travels on to spend the night among his fellow-Israelites in Gibeah. After a disappointingly long wait in the town square for an offer of hospitality, an old man arrives and invites the visitors into his home. They wash their feet and then gather for dinner. As they eat and drink, they're interrupted by a crowd of locals outside:

Judges 19 v 22-30
Pounding on the door, they shouted to the old man who owned the house, "Bring out the man who came to your house so we can have sex with him."

The owner of the house went outside and said to them, "No, my friends, don't be so vile. Since this man is my guest, don't do this disgraceful thing. Look, here is my virgin daughter, and his concubine. I will bring them out to you now, and you can use them and do to them whatever you wish. But to this man, don't do such a disgraceful thing."

But the men would not listen to him. So the man took his concubine and sent her outside to them, and they raped her and abused her throughout the night, and at dawn they let her go. At daybreak the woman went back to the house where her master was staying, fell down at the door and lay there until daylight.

When her master got up in the morning and opened the door of the house and stepped out to continue on his way, there lay his concubine, fallen in the doorway of the house, with her hands on the threshold. He said to her, "Get up; let's go." But there was no answer. Then the man put her on his donkey and set out for home. When he reached home, he took a knife and cut up his concubine, limb by limb, into twelve parts and sent them into all the areas of Israel. Everyone who saw it said, "Such a thing has never been seen or done, not since the day the Israelites came up out of Egypt. Think about it! Consider it! Tell us what to do!"

The writer of Judges gives an answer to the people's howl for guidance. He starts and ends that section of the book with the same comment: "In those days Israel had no king" (19 v 1; 21 v 25). The absence of a king explains why "everyone did what was right in his own eyes" (21 v 25, ESV). It seems that without a king Israel will never honour the covenant.

A king could make all the difference because, with the power of the state at his disposal, he could strong-arm the people into covenant acceptance. And yet a king is just as likely to reject the covenant as the people, which is exactly what happens with Saul, the first king of Israel (see for example 1 Samuel 22 v 17-19). God has to punish Saul and bring his dynasty to an end (1 Samuel 15 v 22-28; 28 v 18-19). With David, however, things truly change for the better. God declares: "I have found David son of Jesse a man after my own heart; he will do everything I want him to do" (Acts 13 v 22). And that's what happens: "The LORD gave David victory everywhere he went. David reigned over all Israel, doing what was just and right for all his people" (1 Chronicles 18 v 13-14). From the people's point of view, "everything the king did pleased them" (2 Samuel 3 v 36). Bearing in mind the dire years described in the book of Judges, this is real progress in redemption history.[60]

From now on, the king's attitude to God determines whether the people get the benefits of covenant acceptance or the troubles of covenant rejection. The welfare of the nation hinges on the king (see for example 2 Kings 21 v 11-12). That's why each king is required to copy out the Law of Moses in his own handwriting, and then read it "all the days of his life" (Deuteronomy 17 v 19). It's why the psalms include numerous prayers for the king (such as Psalm 61 v 6-7). And it's why the prophets focus so much attention on whoever's reigning at the time. But this emphasis on the king doesn't mean the Israelites are barred from all of God's covenant blessings when the king is disobedient. Regardless of the king, the people are accountable for their own personal response to the eternal covenant (see 1 Kings 19 v 14, 18).

God says the house of David will "endure for ever before me" (2 Samuel 7 v 16). Given that the house of Saul didn't even notch up two kings, this is a mind-stretching promise. There are two ways in which it could be fulfilled. Either David's descendants will keep on producing male heirs in an endless chain of succession, or one of them will somehow make the kingdom his own for ever. Even during David's time, it's clear God has the latter in store. David speaks in one of his psalms of a mighty "Lord", carefully distinguishing him from the LORD God:

Psalm 110 v 1-2

The LORD says to my Lord:
"Sit at my right hand
until I make your enemies
a footstool for your feet."
The LORD will extend your mighty sceptre from Zion.

This "Lord" is a king (he has a sceptre, the sign of kingship), and he reigns from Jerusalem (Jerusalem is another name for Zion) over all the earth (verse 6). Surprisingly, David calls him "my Lord". That's remarkable because, as we've just seen, God has told David that the kings reigning in Jerusalem will from now on be his descendants. So why would David bow down to one of his own sons? The explanation comes in verse 4 of the psalm (which, like verse 1, is said by God to the future king): "You are a priest for ever, in the order of Melchizedek." This king is an eternal priest, which means he has "an indestructible life" (Hebrews 7 v 16-17). He'll single-handedly ensure that the house of David is never extinguished. No wonder David kneels before him.

Salvation history is now tied to the kingship of Israel. Only an immortal descendant of David ruling from Jerusalem will satisfy the expectations of Scripture. Since the time of Adam and Eve, the world has been waiting for humanity's promised saviour. Like a police investigation narrowing down the range of suspects, the Bible has now closed in on one family's DNA and one occupation. This future King, known as the "Son of David" (see Matthew 12 v 23) or the "Messiah",[61] is the world's only hope. In the meantime, before his coming, the kings of Israel carry out the vital covenant role set out above. As a result, the history of God's people temporarily becomes a collection of royal biographies.

A house for God

In his book about the decline of Zimbabwe, *When a Crocodile Eats the Sun*, Peter Godwin describes the time when the HIV virus arrived. His mother, a doctor, had to explain what the future would hold to the first patient diagnosed with the virus at her hospital. Their conversation went like this:

"You have a new viral disease that will cause you great difficulties in time. And there is no treatment for it yet."

"But I feel better now."

"Good, just enjoy yourself, while you feel well. Keep as healthy

as you can, eat well, don't get overtired. And I will be at your side."[62]

Dr Godwin was true to those final words. The patient remained under her care until she eventually died from AIDS ten years later. "I will be at your side." Those words would have brought great comfort at such a frightening time. It's difficult to think of anything more valuable during hardship than having someone trustworthy beside you. And even when life is going smoothly, it's good to know a friend is close at hand. The nation of Israel enjoyed this blessing on an extraordinary scale. The Creator God himself accompanied them in the tabernacle. Moses knew exactly what to say to encourage his successor Joshua: "The LORD himself goes before you and will be with you; he will never leave you nor forsake you" (Deuteronomy 31 v 8).

The covenant with David, however, brings about a dramatic change in the way God dwells among the Israelites. God begins with a travelogue:

2 Samuel 7 v 6-7

I have not dwelt in a house from the day I brought the Israelites up out of Egypt to this day. I have been moving from place to place with a tent as my dwelling. Wherever I have moved with all of the Israelites, did I ever say to any of their rulers whom I commanded to shepherd my people Israel, "Why have you not built me a house of cedar?"

Then he says that David's son will be the one who'll "build a house for my Name" (2 Samuel 7 v 13). So God is sending out a change of address card. At this point in history he's moving from "No Fixed Abode" to "The Temple, Mount Moriah, Jerusalem, Israel".

After seven years of building, it's time to transfer the ark from tent to temple:

1 Kings 8 v 1
Then King Solomon summoned into his presence at Jerusalem the elders of Israel, all the heads of the tribes and the chiefs of the Israelite families, to bring up the ark of the LORD's covenant from Zion, the City of David.

We can tell from that verse that the temple has been constructed just outside the original city limits of Jerusalem. The precise site of the temple is an area to the north of Mount Zion (the location of Jerusalem – see 2 Samuel 5 v 6-7) called Mount Moriah (see 2 Chronicles 3 v 1). Once the temple is up and running, the city boundaries spread northwards to encompass it. So the temple becomes part of Jerusalem – and therefore part of "Zion" (see Psalm 20 v 2).

The ark's new address is a significant development. From the moment God relocates to the temple, the major action of salvation history takes place in Jerusalem. Moses had prepared the people for this beforehand:

Deuteronomy 12 v 11-14
Then to the place the LORD your God will choose as a dwelling for his name – there you are to bring everything I command you: your burnt offerings and sacrifices, your tithes and special gifts, and all the choice possessions you have vowed to the LORD. And there rejoice before the LORD your God ... Be careful not to sacrifice your burnt offerings anywhere you please. Offer them only at the place the LORD will choose in one of your tribes, and there observe everything I command you.

This makes Jerusalem the only legitimate venue for the key rituals of the faith of Israel. What's more, as we've already seen, Psalm 110 identifies Jerusalem as the seat of power of the promised Messiah (see also Psalm 2 v 6). Jerusalem, often called "Mount Zion" or just "Zion" in the Bible, now becomes the operations centre for God's work in the world. David sums this up when he says of Mount Zion, "There the LORD bestows his blessing, even life for evermore" (Psalm 133 v 3). The point is spelled out even more clearly by the prophet Joel: "Everyone who calls on the name of the LORD will be saved; for on Mount Zion and in Jerusalem there will be deliverance" (2 v 32).

In the time of Abraham, it was as if God opened Google Earth and then zoomed in on the land of Israel. Now, through the covenant with David, God uses the zoom function again to bring up Jerusalem, a hilltop city so small it could fit nine times inside New York's Central Park. One tiny city will determine the destiny of the whole globe.

Life lessons

- **Jesus was and is the promised King of the covenant with David.** Not only was he one of David's descendants (Luke 3 v 31), he was also officially appointed King of Israel during his time on earth. Israel was at that time part of the Roman Empire, and Pontius Pilate was the governor of the region. So when Pilate declares that Jesus is "King of the Jews" (John 19 v 19-22), the appointment is legally authoritative. The announcement is made on a notice attached to a large wooden cross on the outskirts of Jerusalem. The newly-appointed King is stripped naked and nails are driven deeply through his hands and feet into the wood of the cross. Jesus' throne is a vicious instrument of execution.

Jesus had said beforehand, looking ahead to his crucifixion: "I, when I am lifted up from the earth, will draw all men to myself" (John 12 v 32; see also v 33). Through the cross, King Jesus wins for himself a population so large that it cannot be counted, made up not only of Israelites but also of people from every nation, tribe and language. They're drawn to him because his crucifixion solves the problem of their sin, providing forgiveness and eternal life. To the scornful passers-by, Jesus' reign as the King of the Jews lasts for only a few powerless, insignificant hours. In reality Jesus is gathering a multitude of followers, and he'll reign over them for ever.

Have you joined his population yet? If you haven't, wouldn't it be wise for you to join his kingdom? Jesus' ancestor David first came to Israel's attention when he defeated Goliath in the Valley of Elah. On that day the Israelite forces were lined up behind him while the Philistines stood behind Goliath on the other side of the valley. All those behind David ended the day victorious; those behind Goliath were slain. It's as if Jesus, "Great David's Greater Son", now stands in David's place and he's beckoning you to join him. Don't stay among the doomed Philistine forces. Cross over to Jesus' side. Do it today.

- Atheists often say that "faith" means trusting in God without evidence.[63] **But in fact the Bible presents countless reasons to believe.** One of the most persuasive is the extraordinary way in which Jesus matches up to the prophecies about the Messiah.[64] We've already seen that God promised David an immortal descendant who would rule from Jerusalem over all the earth. After David's time, the prophets added many further details about the Messiah. Isaiah, for example, says that a king "on David's throne" (Isaiah 9 v 7) would be called "Mighty God" (9 v 6) and would be "a great light" in "Galilee of the Gentiles" (9 v 1-2), bringing eternal peace (9 v 7). Later Isaiah speaks of God's "servant", who must be the same person as the king of chapter 9 because he too is a "light for the Gentiles" who will save the world (see 49 v 6). Yet this glorious servant king will be "despised and abhorred by the nation" (49 v 7). A few chapters later, Isaiah returns to the theme of the "servant", who is "despised and rejected by men" (52 v 13; 53 v 3). Despite his innocence (53 v 9), he'll be brutally put to death: "He was pierced for our transgressions ... cut off from the land of the living" (53 v 5, 8). Yet we're told that "after the suffering of his soul, he will see the light" (53 v 11). These unthinkable combinations – majesty and disgust, power and suffering, divinity and punishment; execution and resurrection – are perfectly fulfilled in Jesus. Even the method of killing, a form of capital punishment that hadn't been invented in Isaiah's day, is correctly foreseen.

The wonder of prediction-fulfilment has been granted by God to give us confidence in him and his works. He has even preserved a manuscript of Isaiah that was written a hundred years before Jesus' birth, part of which is on permanent display at the Israel Museum in Jerusalem. As he says in Isaiah 46 v 9-10, "I am God and there is no other; I am God, and there is none like me. I make known the end from the beginning, from ancient times, what is still to come." Atheists may choose to disregard the evidence, but they have no right to claim that none has been provided.

• **Both elements of the covenant with David are brought together in the person of Jesus.** He's not only the promised "Son of David" (Matthew 1 v 1), he's also the new temple:

> ### John 2 v 18-22
> Then the Jews demanded of him, "What miraculous sign can you show us to prove your authority to do all this?" Jesus answered them, "Destroy this temple, and I will raise it again in three days."
> The Jews replied, "It has taken forty-six years to build this temple, and you are going to raise it in three days?" But the temple he had spoken of was his body. After he was raised from the dead, his disciples recalled what he had said. Then they believed the Scripture and the words that Jesus had spoken.

Jesus refers to himself as the temple because he's taken over the temple's role as the go-to place for worshiping God. Visiting the temple in Jerusalem was once the only way to worship the Creator. That's why the Israelites called on the rest of the world to come to their temple to worship God (see Psalm 96 v 7-9; Psalm 100 v 1, 4). But now we bring our offerings to God through Jesus (Hebrews 13 v 15-16).

So God's people in new covenant times have a different announcement for the nations: they can worship God right where they are, through the risen Jesus. What a privilege to take that message to a nation or tribe or neighbourhood where Jesus is not yet known! What beautiful feet belong to those who proclaim the good news (Isaiah 52 v 7) – whether in distant lands or close to home! Not everyone is cut out to be a missionary or evangelist (see Ephesians 4 v 11). But every Christian can, and should, play *some* part in the Great Commission (Matthew 28 v 18-20).[65]

Chapter 9

The New Covenant:

"Better promises" (Hebrews 8 v 6)

The story so far

Under the first covenant, mankind was given the high privilege of acting as God's viceroys in the world. Through marriage they could populate the earth. The Sabbath offered weekly refreshment. But Adam and Eve ate from the forbidden tree, rejecting God's generous and loving provision. With amazing mercy, God decreed that a future saviour, one of Eve's descendants, would restore mankind's fortunes. When this second covenant was cold-shouldered, God flooded the world, saving only Noah and his family. The covenant with Noah ensured the world's protection in the future. But the Tower of Babel demonstrated hostility towards God and brought about his judgment on humanity. God then revealed to Abraham that he would father a nation and inherit the land of Canaan. After the exodus of Abraham's descendants from Egypt, God led them to the promised land. He set out his legal code through the covenant with Moses and dwelt among his people in the tabernacle. But the Israelites rebelled, and so God punished them through foreign invaders, who took away the ark of the covenant. God then graciously raised up David to lead Israel into covenant faithfulness. The ark was restored to its central place in Israel's worship. A sixth covenant promised an enduring dynasty for David and a temple in Jerusalem for God.

Introducing the new covenant

After a bright dawn in the first years of David's reign, and a period of splendour under Solomon, the kingdom of Israel breaks into two. Ten of the Israelite tribes rebel against King Rehoboam, Solomon's son, and form their own northern kingdom (taking the name "Israel" with them). Rehoboam's own tribe, Judah, stays loyal to him as king, as does the tribe of Benjamin (1 Kings 12 v 21). They form the southern kingdom of Judah. Things look bad for the northern tribes right from the start. By rejecting Rehoboam, they're distancing themselves from the eternal covenant, with its promises about the house of David (see 1 Kings 12 v 19). Then there's a further slide when King Jeroboam, their first king, deliberately ignores the temple clause in the covenant with David. He doesn't want his people making regular trips to the temple in Rehoboam's kingdom, so he sets up two centres for offering sacrifices in his northern kingdom (1 Kings 12 v 27-30). In this way he stirs up the same kind of idolatrous calf worship that caused so much trouble during the time of Moses and Aaron. Many of the kings of Israel then encourage additional kinds of disobedience, despite warnings from prophets such as Elijah, Elisha, Amos, and Hosea. Ultimately, in 722 BC, Israel is conquered by the Assyrians. The people are forced into exile and scattered (2 Kings 17 v 23).

Meanwhile, in the south, the record of the kings of Judah is patchy. While some receive the Bible's praise – like Josiah, Asa, and Hezekiah – the majority lead God's people into idol worship. Manasseh is probably the most disobedient of all the kings of Judah: "In both courts of the temple of the LORD, he built altars to all the starry hosts. He sacrificed his own son in the fire, practised sorcery and divination, and consulted mediums and spiritists. He did much evil in the eyes of the LORD, provoking him to anger" (2 Kings 21 v 5-6). God's response is firm and final:

2 Kings 21 v 11-15

Manasseh king of Judah has committed these detestable sins. He has done more evil than the Amorites who preceded him and has led Judah into sin with his idols. Therefore this is what the LORD, the God of Israel, says: I am going to bring such disaster on Jerusalem and Judah that the ears of everyone who hears of it will tingle. I will stretch out over Jerusalem the measuring line used against Samaria and the plumb-line used against the house of Ahab. I will wipe out Jerusalem as one wipes out a dish, wiping it and turning it upside-down. I will forsake the remnant of my inheritance and hand them over to their enemies. They will be looted and plundered by all their foes, because they have done evil in my eyes and have provoked me to anger from the day their forefathers came out of Egypt until this day.

The prophecy is fulfilled through three separate invasions by the Babylonians, in 605, 597 and 586 BC (Daniel 1 v 1-5; 2 Kings 24 v 8-17; 2 Kings 25 v 8-11). Judah is defeated. The city of Jerusalem and the temple are destroyed. The people are carried away into exile. For Jeremiah, it's as if the world has been uncreated. He uses the language of Genesis 1 v 2, before the first day of creation week: "I looked at the earth, and it was formless and empty; and at the heavens, and their light was gone … I looked, and the fruitful land was a desert; all its towns lay in ruins before the LORD, before his fierce anger" (Jeremiah 4 v 23, 26).

The desolation of the Jewish exiles still reaches out to us, like the tolling of a distant bell:

Psalm 137 v 1, ESV

By the waters of Babylon
there we sat down and wept,
when we remembered Zion.

Their tears are understandable. The exiles are no longer ruled by a king from David's line, and they can no longer worship the LORD at the temple in Jerusalem. Both of the distinctive features of the covenant with David appear to have been terminated. This leads the psalm-writer to raise a profound question: "How can we sing the songs of the LORD while in a foreign land?" (verse 4). To put the question another way, how can the exiles maintain covenant relationship with God when that doesn't seem possible any more? The answer comes in the very next line: "If I forget you, O Jerusalem, may my right hand forget its skill" (verse 5). The exiles need to trust that Jerusalem – the chosen venue for eternal deliverance – will rise from the ashes.

That longing is partially fulfilled in 538 BC when Cyrus of Persia orders the rebuilding of the temple in Jerusalem and allows the exiles to return (2 Chronicles 36 v 22-23). But the kingship remains in foreign hands. Without a son of David reigning over them, there's a sense in which the people are still in exile. They're "slaves" in their own land (Ezra 9 v 9; Nehemiah 9 v 36-37).[66] That's why, in the books of the Old Testament written after the return from Babylon, we often find the people of God in distress. But alongside the hardship, there's great hope for the future, based on God's pledge to "raise up from David's line a righteous Branch, a King who will reign wisely and do what is just and right in the land" (Jeremiah 23 v 5, see NIV footnote). God's King is coming. On the salvation history timeline, his arrival will be another re-ignition for the people of God. And in

God-given conscience. So the new covenant's
 must be similar to the conscience but more
a deeper incision of the divine stylus. The
iel gives us further details. He says that the
 will exert his mighty influence on the heart:
 the Sovereign LORD says ... I will give you a
I will put my Spirit in you and move you to
rees and be careful to keep my laws" (Ezekiel
7). Like a super-strong conscience, the Spirit
e sinful desires of the heart.

influence on new covenant believers' hearts
way the need for written law, as we can tell
f the quotation from Ezekiel above. The Bible
main weapon against the sin factory beating
d. He uses it to judge "the thoughts and
 heart" (Hebrews 4 v 12).

ntroduction of the Spirit's permanent heart
ord of God's people was more often than not
or. Afterwards, things improve dramatically.
any in the Corinthian church fail badly (1
 v 17); the Galatians are quick to swallow
Galatians 3 v 1); some of the Thessalonians
salonians 3 v 11); and the believers written
 guilty of favouring the rich (James 2 v
misdeeds are not on the same scale as the
der the old covenant, and the offenders
sive to criticism from God's spokesmen
 2 Corinthians 7 v 8-16). Generally in the
we find new covenant people serving God
leheartedly and effectively. God has truly
 deeply into their hearts, by his Spirit.[68]

keeping with the usual pattern, it will be accompanied by
a covenant:

Jeremiah 31 v 31
"The time is coming," declares the LORD,
"when I will make a new covenant
 with the house of Israel
 and with the house of Judah."

After that prophecy, six centuries pass by before the King
appears, bringing with him the promised covenant. But
while God's people wait, they can consult Jeremiah's
detailed blueprint of the covenant that's on the way
(Jeremiah 31 v 31-34). It will offer new power, form a new
people and grant new peace.

A new power
In Nairobi, Kenya, in February 2005, Sundeep Hunjan was
driving back from work with her father. "It was a Monday.
It was a very hot day and we were driving home with the
windows open. We were in traffic, and just as we started
moving, I felt something hot pour over me. I didn't know
what it was. I got out of the car, but I couldn't see anything.
Then my father told me it was acid." The attacker – still
unknown – left Sundeep with severely disfiguring third-
degree burns on her face and torso. Her eyelids could
no longer cover her eyes. Half of the hair on the side of
her head was burned away. Sundeep had been due to get
married two months later. From her hospital bed she said:
"You just wonder why."[67]

The Bible answers that haunting question. Evil deeds can
be traced back to the human heart: "The heart is deceitful
above all things and beyond cure" (Jeremiah 17 v 9). It

seems no desire is so wicked that it cannot find a home in the human heart. Jesus tells us, "From within, out of men's hearts, come evil thoughts, sexual immorality, theft, murder, adultery, greed, malice, deceit, lewdness, envy, slander, arrogance and folly. All these evils come from inside" (Mark 7 v 21-23). The heart is a hard-working and productive sin factory. Ever since Eden we've followed our first parents in rejecting God's knowledge of good and evil. As a result our hearts have an "anything goes" approach. While God mercifully provides barriers like the conscience (Romans 2 v 14-15), and national laws (Romans 13 v 2-4), sometimes the human heart pushes a person all the way through to acts of great depravity, such as throwing acid into the face of a defenceless woman. As has often been said, the heart of the human problem is the problem of the human heart.

This heart condition explains why Israel keeps turning away from God, despite his kindness and goodness. The eternal covenant calls for sincere willingness to obey God, and that's incompatible with the "anything goes" policy of the heart. In the previous chapter we saw that having a king as covenant enforcer did sometimes have a positive effect. The godly kings led the people into greater obedience than Israel had known since Joshua's day. But in the pages of Israel's history there aren't many godly monarchs. Most of the kings give way to the sinful desires of their own mutinous hearts. And even when a godly king is on the throne, there's no guarantee that the people will submit to his rule (see for example 2 Samuel 15 v 10-14).

Given Israel's record under the kings, something clearly needs to be done about the human heart if salvation history is going to move forward. In God's wisdom the new covenant prophesied by Jeremiah has a highly effective

strategy for dealing wit
into the cardiology dep
divine specialist is read
their trays, and the first
upon the table. Spirit
place:

Jeremiah 31 v 31-33
Behold, the days are
make a new covenant
of Judah, not like the
on the day when I to
of the land of Egypt,
was their husband, d
that I will make wi
declares the LORD: I
write it on their hea
be my people.

The Ten Command
into two tablets of
were a wonderful
the people becaus
into the hearts the
and I will write it
this treatment wi

There's anothe
of heart-writing.
have the law, do
they show that t
their hearts, the
defending them
law is already w

through our
heart-writing
powerful –
prophet Eze
Spirit of God
"This is wha
new heart…
follow my de
36 v 22, 26-2
overpowers th

The Spirit's
doesn't take
from the end
is the Spirit's
within manki
attitudes of th

Before the
surgery, the re
unspeakably p
It's true that
Corinthians 1
false teaching
are lazy (2 The
to by James a
1-6). But these
worst abuses u
are more respo
(see for exampl
New Testament
sacrificially, wh
inscribed his law

A new people

Schools always seem to have an "in-crowd". To belong you need to wear the right clothes and (even more importantly) the right shoes, have the right kind of hairstyle, and listen to the right music. But even checking all those boxes won't necessarily get someone accepted. No one considered dull or overly keen to impress has much of a chance. According to the Bible, God also has an in-crowd. But membership has nothing to do with fashion sense. From the start of history onwards, membership of God's people has always been an undeserved privilege granted by God.

Before the new covenant, God's people were a mixed bag: some trusting in him, others rejecting him. That meant true covenant believers sometimes felt completely isolated, despite living among God's chosen people. Here's the minority report that Elijah presents to God:

1 Kings 19 v 14

I have been very zealous for the LORD God Almighty. The Israelites have rejected your covenant, broken down your altars, and put your prophets to death with the sword. I am the only one left, and now they are trying to kill me too.

He's told in response that in fact there's a significant remnant of believers: "I reserve seven thousand in Israel – all whose knees have not bowed down to Baal and all whose mouths have not kissed him" (1 Kings 19 v 18). But from Elijah's point of view, he's living among God's people without knowing any other true believer.

Jeremiah predicts that a time is coming when God's people won't be mixed in this way: "'No longer will a man teach his neighbour, or a man his brother, saying, "Know the LORD," because they will all know me, from the least of them to the greatest,' declares the LORD" (Jeremiah 31 v 34). Under the old covenant, Elijah has to tell King Ahab to "know the LORD" (see 1 Kings 18 v 18-19), even though Ahab, as an Israelite, already belongs to the people of God. In the time of the new covenant, however, membership of God's people is only for genuine covenant believers. They don't need to be told to "know the LORD" because they know him already.

Sometimes Christians have thought of the new covenant people of God as a *replacement* for the Jewish people. Yet Paul points out that there's a remnant of Jewish believers in new covenant times, echoing the remnant of Elijah's day (Romans 11 v 1-5). This shows that "God did not reject his people" (11 v 2). In fact, the new covenant church is pictured in the book of Romans as a *Jewish* tree with lots of wild Gentile branches grafted in (11 v 24).[69] So instead of "replacement theology" this is "enlargement theology". However, it's sad but true to say that at the time of the new covenant's introduction, many unbelieving Jewish

Diagram 2: The People of God
(before and after the new covenant):

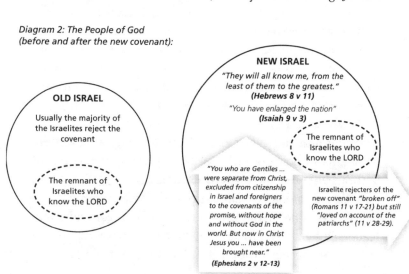

OLD ISRAEL

Usually the majority of the Israelites reject the covenant

The remnant of Israelites who know the LORD

NEW ISRAEL

"They will all know me, from the least of them to the greatest."
(Hebrews 8 v 11)

"You have enlarged the nation"
(Isaiah 9 v 3)

The remnant of Israelites who know the LORD

"You who are Gentiles ... were separate from Christ, excluded from citizenship in Israel and foreigners to the covenants of the promise, without hope and without God in the world. But now in Christ Jesus you ... have been brought near."
(Ephesians 2 v 12-13)

Israelite rejecters of the new covenant "broken off" (Romans 11 v 17-21) but still "loved on account of the patriarchs" (11 v 28-29).

branches are broken off (11 v 17). Membership of God's people becomes dependent on faith in God's promises.

The term "Israel" continues to be used as a way of talking about God's people, despite the reconfiguration brought about by the new covenant. Paul describes all those who have been born again, whether Jew or Gentile, as "the Israel of God" (Galatians 6 v 15-16).[70] But it's important to note that the physical descendants of old covenant Israel – the Jews – are also called "Israel" in the New Testament (Romans 9 v 4; 11 v 11). This double usage of the term means we need to identify carefully which Israel the New Testament writers have in mind.[71] On one occasion Paul even brings both uses of "Israel" together in a single sentence when he says: "Not all who are descended from Israel are Israel" (Romans 9 v 6)!

While it's clear that God no longer considers unbelieving Jews to be his people in the way they once were (as we saw above, they've been broken off the tree), he still has a special love for them. There's a sense in which they're still chosen:

Romans 11 v 28-29

As far as the gospel is concerned they are enemies on your account; but as far as election is concerned, they are loved on account of the patriarchs, for God's gifts and his call are irrevocable.

No other race has ever received this irrevocable "election" or "call" – only the Jewish people. That explains why Paul, despite being the apostle to the Gentiles, says to the Jews of Pisidian Antioch: "We had to speak the word of God to you first" (Acts 13 v 46). When God sees Jewish non-believers, he remembers their fathers – Abraham, Isaac and Jacob –

and his heart is filled with a special longing for them to hear the gospel.

A new peace

The Forth Bridge, a railway bridge near Edinburgh linking south-east and north-east Scotland, was built between 1883 and 1890. It's still considered a marvel of engineering. It's one and a half miles long, and made from 55,000 tons of steel, held in place by eight million rivets (the last rivet was hammered home by the Prince of Wales at the opening ceremony, and was gold-plated in honour of the occasion). Keeping the paintwork of the Forth Bridge in good condition is obviously a challenging task. Over the years a myth has grown up that whenever the bridge has finally been repainted, the workers immediately have to go back to the beginning and start all over again. Whether or not that's ever really been the case, the idea has caught on. When faced with a never-ending task people say: "It's like painting the Forth Bridge."

The sacrificial system of the old covenant was like painting the Forth Bridge. The work of the priests was never finished. There were always further sacrifices to be made. Something of the endless, wearisome nature of the task comes across in a line from the book of Hebrews. We're told the high priest would offer "sacrifices day after day, first for his own sins, and then for the sins of the people" (Hebrews 7 v 27). Under the old covenant, each new day brought a fresh round of bleating goats and lowing bulls into the temple courts. As Ray Galea says: "The temple was more like an abattoir than a museum or a cathedral."[72] The ceaseless sacrificing made it obvious that sin had not been dealt with in a final way (Hebrews 10 v 1-2).

But Jeremiah says that a time is coming when the temple's

sacrificial system will no longer be necessary. God reveals to him that the new covenant will bring full, lasting forgiveness: "I will forgive their wickedness and will remember their sins no more" (Jeremiah 31 v 34). The book of Hebrews explains how this prophecy is fulfilled: "[Christ] has appeared once for all at the end of the ages to do away with sin by the sacrifice of himself" (Hebrews 9 v 26). Jesus' blood, worth so much more than the blood of goats and bulls, successfully pays the penalty. His blood offers complete relief to our heavy-burdened consciences (Hebrews 9 v 14; 10 v 14, 22). God's love for those who take part in his eternal covenant is so great that he himself comes down to be our substitute, in the person of his Son. His body is torn on the cross, as he takes the curse for covenant failure in our place. He spares us the wrathful curse we deserve. It's no wonder believers can't stop singing about a brutal execution in the Middle East that happened 2000 years ago.

The signs of the new covenant

The covenant with Noah led to the stunning sight of a rainbow set among the clouds. It was given as a sign of God's commitment to preserve the world, a memory aid reassuring covenant believers that the world would never be destroyed again. In a similar way, circumcision was the sign of the covenant with Abraham. It reminded him of the need for ruthlessness with sin. The new covenant has two signs representing important spiritual truths: the Lord's Supper and baptism.

The first ever Lord's Supper takes place during Jesus' final evening with his disciples, where he himself explains its meaning:

Luke 22 v 19-20

And he took bread, gave thanks and broke it, and gave it to them, saying, "This is my body given for you; do this in *remembrance* of me." In the same way, after the supper he took the cup, saying, "This cup is the new covenant in my blood, which is poured out for you."

So the body-like bread and blood-like wine of the Lord's Supper help us to keep on remembering Jesus' death. The Lord's Supper is also a way of proclaiming the importance of Jesus' death: Paul says, "Whenever you eat this bread and drink this cup, you *proclaim* the Lord's death until he comes" (1 Corinthians 11 v 26). It's naturally a time for "*thanksgiving*" (1 Corinthians 10 v 16). But that's still not all, because Paul goes on to describe the Lord's Supper as a "*participation* in the blood of Christ" and a "*participation* in the body of Christ" (1 Corinthians 10 v 16). That's because we demonstrate to God our saving faith in the cross when we eat the bread and drink the wine with sincere hearts. Four words: remembrance; proclamation; thanksgiving; and participation sum up the rich significance of this simple meal.

Baptism symbolises the spiritual clean-up brought about by Jesus' death and resurrection when someone is united with him through faith (see Acts 22 v 16 and Romans 6 v 3-7, both discussed below). Jesus makes it a sign of the new covenant when he tells his disciples:

Matthew 28 v 18-20

All authority in heaven and on earth has been given to me. Therefore go and make disciples of all nations, baptising them in the name of the Father and of the Son and of the Holy Spirit, and teaching them to obey everything I have commanded you. And surely I am with you always, to the very end of the age.

The order is significant. When Jesus sets out the disciple-making process, he puts baptism before instruction. This implies that baptism is an "entry sign", like the ultra-violet marks stamped on people's wrists when they enter a music festival. The book of Acts seems to confirm this. Throughout Acts people are baptised as soon as they join God's new covenant people. Luke writes that after Peter's evangelistic sermon in Jerusalem, "Those who accepted his message were baptised, and about three thousand were added to their number that day" (Acts 2 v 41). The Ethiopian eunuch is also baptised as soon as he accepts the covenant message (Acts 8 v 35-38). And a whole family are baptised on the very same night that they hear and believe the good news about Jesus (Acts 16 v 32-34).

This assumption that baptism happens at the start of the Christian life is also seen when Paul tells the Roman believers that they were "baptised into Christ" (Romans 6 v 3). In other words, when they were baptised they were submerged not just into water but also into Jesus – because they were saying yes, *through their baptism*, to what God offers in Jesus (see also 1 Peter 3 v 18-22, especially v 21). That's the reason why Ananias tells Paul, "Be baptised and wash your sins away" (Acts 22 v 16). He's encouraging Paul to come to Jesus, and he's presenting baptism, the sign of that cleansing union, as the way in.[73]

- One of the most encouraging moments in the whole Bible is when Peter promises that everyone who repents and is baptised will receive "the gift of the Holy Spirit" (Acts 2 v 38). Sometimes we fail to grasp just how helpless we would be without this gift. Jesus says: "Apart from me you can do nothing" (John 15 v 5), which is very humbling. He says it because we have a powerful enemy. We also have hearts that still naturally veer towards evil (Matthew 7 v 11; Romans 7 v 19). And we have imperfect knowledge, which means it's easy for us to make chronic mistakes. These things and others are stacked against us.

  We need the help of the "Spirit of Christ" (Romans 8 v 9). The way to experience his powerful help can be summed up in one word: prayerfulness. Jesus loves to help his people through his Spirit – the Bible says he is "full of grace" (John 1 v 14). But he helps those who ask: "You do not have, because you do not ask God" (James 4 v 2); "Ask and it will be given to you" (Luke 11 v 9); "If you believe, you will receive whatever you ask for in prayer" (Matthew 21 v 22). We need to ask the Spirit to help us – and we need his Scriptures to know what to ask for. Lack of dependence on God leads to ineffectiveness. Good intentions and gifts count for nothing. We need power from God (Zechariah 4 v 6). And that calls for prayer.

- As we've seen, in old covenant days the people of God were a mixture of covenant accepters and rejecters. So there were times when believers like Elijah didn't know where to go to find fellowship. In our day it's so much easier to locate believers and meet up with them because God's people now gather on the basis of faith, not nationality. The Bible expects us to do all we can to join a local church that holds firmly to the new covenant, and then get fully involved. One among many verses that make this point is 1 Peter 1 v 22, which literally says: "Having purified yourselves through obedience of the truth *into* sincere brotherly love, love one another earnestly from the heart." In other words, **those who accept the truth about Jesus are plunged into a new relationship of brotherly love with one another.** This is something we ought to rejoice in and give ourselves to eagerly, as commanded by the second half of the verse. It's fair to say that many believers in the west try to commit as little as possible to their local church. We've swallowed the modern world's lie that the best way to live is to be free of responsibilities. But we know from normal family life that things are best when everyone spends plenty of time together, and when each family member helps out with the chores. It's no different with Jesus' family (Mark 3 v 34-35).

• Paul says of Israel: "I ask then: did God reject his people? By no means! I am an Israelite myself, a descendant of Abraham" (Romans 11 v 1). He goes on to speak of God's particular concern for unbelieving Jewish people (11 v 28-29). To be godly is to be like God, and this is an area of life where we need to resemble the "God of Abraham, Isaac and Jacob" (Acts 3 v 13). He earnestly desires the "heirs ... of the covenant" (3 v 25) to receive the blessings of covenant fulfilment in Jesus. He says: "O Israel, I will not forget you ... Can a mother forget the baby at her breast, and have no compassion on the child she has borne? Though she may forget, I will not forget you! See, I have engraved you on the palms of my hands" (Isaiah 44 v 21; 49 v 15-16). The Jewish people's survival is a remarkable fact, given that for most of the past two thousand years they've had no land to call their own, and have faced the most vicious persecutors in all of human history. God's preservation of Abraham's descendants fulfils the Scriptures that speak of their ongoing presence in the world (such as Romans 11 v 25), and gives us the opportunity to reach them with the good news of their Messiah. **Every believer can contribute to the evangelisation of the Jewish people,** whether through prayer, giving, or personal involvement in outreach efforts. Hudson Taylor took this principle of godliness to heart. Despite the huge demands of missionary work in inland China in the nineteenth century, year after year he sent financial support to the Mildmay Mission to the Jews in London. He did what he could – is that currently true of you?

- **The Lord's Supper is a group thing.** There's no indication in the Bible that it's ever right to eat the bread and drink the wine by oneself. This is still further proof that we're saved into a community. And since we can't celebrate the Lord's Supper with all believers everywhere, it demonstrates the truth that God has organised his universal church (Colossians 1 v 18) into local churches (Colossians 4 v 15-16). In this way the ceremony compels those who want its benefits to join a local church. God has tied this covenant sign to membership of his new community – we cannot have the former without the latter. The Lord's Supper makes the individualistic approach to Christianity impossible.

- Christian disagreement concerning the baptism of believers' newborn children will no doubt continue until Jesus returns. Since the debate isn't going away, we should resolve to conduct it graciously: "Everyone should be quick to listen, slow to speak and slow to become angry" (James 1 v 19). It's especially important that both sides recognise the sincerity of their opponents. We might reach different conclusions about what the Bible says, but we share the same inward desire to honour God by putting his word into practice. The roll-call of church history includes spiritual giants from both camps. C.H. Spurgeon's spirit of charity sets a good example for us all: himself a Baptist, he was nonetheless willing to appoint a man who believed in baptising church babies as the first principal of his Pastors' College.[74]

  The Bible's covenants provide both sides of the baptism debate with scriptural arguments to back up their case. Those who say that it's wrong to baptise believers' babies could point to the reconfiguration of God's people under the new covenant. Since God's people now gather on the basis of faith, not race, it can be argued that baptism should be delayed until there has been clear expression and evidence of faith. Those on the opposite side could highlight the correlation between baptism and circumcision – they both seem to be covenant entry signs. If it was right in old covenant times to welcome babies into the covenant family and raise them as covenant believers, it can be argued that we should do the same in new covenant times.

- At the start of this book we saw that a covenant is

an agreement establishing a relationship, with life or death consequences. Throughout salvation history no one has lived the blameless life required for covenant relationship with God (Genesis 17 v 1; Psalm 15). But all through the Bible we see sinful people agreeing to the covenant available to them at the time, and then enjoying relationship with God as a result. Their grievous shortcomings, such as David's adulterous relationship with Bathsheba and his murder of her husband, don't bring their friendship with God to an end. It's true that the sacrificial system offers a limited explanation for this state of affairs. But it can still seem that God doesn't take the "blamelessness clause" of his covenant seriously. The crucifixion of Jesus, the second person of the Trinity, ties all of these loose threads together. It reveals how God can "be just and the one who justifies those who have faith in Jesus" (Romans 3 v 26). At the cross, God takes upon himself the covenant penalty incurred by all covenant believers throughout all time. The sacrificial blood poured out by Jesus is "the blood of the eternal covenant" (Hebrews 13 v 20). No one could ever have been in covenant relationship with God without it. Through the cross, all of the covenants literally bleed into one (Hebrews 9 v 15).

The cross has many life lessons to teach. But perhaps humility is one that modern believers particularly need to take to heart. John Stott puts the point like this:

> *Every time we look at the cross Christ seems to say to us, "I am here because of you. It is your sin I am bearing, your curse I am suffering, your debt I am paying, your death I am dying." Nothing in history or in the universe cuts us*

down to size like the cross. All of us have inflated views
of ourselves, especially in self-righteousness, until we have
visited a place called Calvary. It is there, at the foot of the
cross, that we shrink to our true size.[75]

Put bluntly, we are not worthy of the covenant blessings we enjoy. "While we were still sinners, Christ died for us" (Romans 5 v 8). This is something we can know in our heads while not knowing it in our hearts. Whenever we think or act with pride, we're forgetting about the cross. We need to learn to "walk humbly" with God (Micah 6 v 8), because of what it cost God to bring us into step beside him.

- **The new covenant doesn't remove law from the Christian life.** God saves people from covenant failures but not from defiant covenant rejection (Numbers 15 v 30-31), and refusing to obey his commands is a way of rejecting the covenant relationship. Jesus says: "If anyone does not remain in me, he is like a branch that is thrown away and withers; such branches are picked up, thrown into the fire and burned" (John 15 v 6; see also Hebrews 10 v 26-31). One aspect of remaining in Jesus, as he himself says, is obeying his commands (John 15 v 10). Obedience does not earn salvation – it's achieved through Jesus' death, from first to last. But the Bible says those who are saved will obey God by the Spirit's power (Romans 8 v 5-9). If you think about it, that's a warning against complacent sinning. As we've seen throughout this book, the covenants require an ongoing commitment to blamelessness.

   In the twenty-first century west, it seems church leaders sometimes overlook the significance of God's law. For example, a blog post on a (usually excellent) Christian website ends: "Jesus fulfilled all of God's perfect conditions so that our relationship to God could be perfectly unconditional. You're free!" In one sense that is wonderfully true: God looks at his covenant people through blood-tinted spectacles because of Jesus, and he delights in us as his fully-forgiven and dearly-loved children. But it strongly implies that we're free to live as we choose, and it's dangerous to give that impression. God's blood-tinted spectacles don't stop him from seeing the way we live, and the way we live matters to him. It matters so much that he has to treat sustained, unrepentant disobedience as covenant rejection (Galatians 5 v 21). That is why Paul says, "I am not free from God's law" (1 Corinthians 9 v 21). Spirit-powered obedience is a necessary consequence of the gospel that saves (1 John 3 v 6-10).[76] Under the new covenant, church leaders are obliged to teach God's commands (Matthew 28 v 20).

- When the people of Israel returned from Babylon, it was only a partial end to their exile. They remained under the control of foreign kings. The arrival of Jesus, the Son of David, was a huge step towards the end of exile, but Jesus didn't bring about full restoration at that time. This can be seen from a conversation between the disciples and the risen Jesus at the start of Acts:

Acts 1 v 6-7
So when they met together they asked him, "Lord, are you at this time going to restore the kingdom to Israel?" He said to them: "It is not for you to know the times or dates the Father has set by his own authority."

The disciples often get things wrong but this time their question is a fair one. About a month beforehand, Jesus had told them that they would "eat and drink at my table in my kingdom and sit on thrones, judging [i.e. governing] the twelve tribes of Israel" (Luke 22 v 30). They're simply asking if the time has come for that promise to be fulfilled.[77] But Jesus says they need to wait until the date set by the Father – who hasn't disclosed its timing (Matthew 24 v 36). It's only when Jesus returns to judge the earth (2 Thessalonians 1 v 7-10) that the people of God will no longer be "exiles" (1 Peter 1 v 1, ESV), "aliens and strangers in the world" (1 Peter 2 v 11), "scattered among the nations" (James 1 v 1). We're not home yet, and we won't be home until Jesus is reigning over us in the new Jerusalem (Revelation 22 v 3).

So believers should have an exile mentality: not overly preoccupied with the world in its current form, where we live in nations that are hostile to God, and our hearts continue to manufacture evil desires, and we suffer the inescapable hardships of the fall. Paul says: "Those who use the things of the world should not become attached to them. For this world as we know it will soon pass away" (1 Corinthians 7 v 31, NLT). How attached are you to the things of this world? Peter says: "Set your hope fully on the grace to be given you when Jesus Christ is revealed" (1 Peter 1 v 13). Is Jesus' return the biggest and brightest thing on your hope-horizon? One way for us to increase our longing for that day is to meditate on the sayings known as "the Beatitudes" in Matthew 5 v 3-12, which contrast the trials of this age with the glories to come. Jesus could arrive at any time, and he will bring our exile to an end. At last we will be home.

Part Three

Reading Scripture the Covenant Way

Chapter 10

The Book of the Covenant

There's a simple reason why it's challenging to read the Bible. Although it was written *for us*, it wasn't written *to us*. We know the whole Bible was written *for* us because Paul says: "All Scripture is God-breathed and is useful for teaching, rebuking, correcting and training in righteousness, so that the man of God may be thoroughly equipped for every good work" (2 Timothy 3 v 16-17; see also 1 Corinthians 9 v 9-10 and 10 v 11). But getting at that usefulness isn't always straightforward, because every book of the Bible was written *to* other people. So we need to think ourselves into their ~~shoes~~ sandals. We can only understand the message *for us now* once we've grasped the message *to them then*.

One example should prove the point. Early on in the book of Revelation there are letters to seven different churches, dictated to John by the ascended Jesus. The letter to the church in Ephesus says: "Remember the height from which you have fallen! Repent and do the things you did at first" (Revelation 2 v 5). But the letter to the church in Thyatira says: "I know your deeds, your love and faith, your service and perseverance, and that you are now doing more than you did at first" (Revelation 2 v 19). If we read Revelation chapter 2 as if it were written to us it would make no sense at all. We'd receive a rebuke for recent spiritual decline, followed immediately by praise for recent spiritual progress. Our Bible-reading session would be a confusing rollercoaster ride. We ought to wait patiently until we've understood the message to them before bridging the gap between then and now so that we can get hold of God's message for us.

The covenants are essential for both parts of the process: grasping the original message and then bridging the gap. Take the fierce closing lines of Psalm 137, quoted earlier in this book:

Psalm 137 v 8-9
O Daughter of Babylon, doomed to destruction,
happy is he who repays you
for what you have done to us –
he who seizes your infants
and dashes them against the rocks.

As we saw in the previous chapter, the psalm is set in exile in Babylon, during the time of the covenant with David. That covenant made provision for God's people to be ruled in the land of Israel by kings from David's line. The Israelites were expected to use the same merciless force in protecting their land as when first gaining possession of it. They acted on God's behalf, carrying out his righteous judgment on sinful, hostile nations (Genesis 15 v 16; 1 Samuel 15 v 2-3; 17 v 45-46), because God's justice is not always postponed until the last day (see also Acts 5 v 1-11; 12 v 23; Romans 1 v 18).

However, in 586 BC the Babylonians defeated God's people, chaining them up and forcing them out of their homeland. In view of these events, the psalm-writer longs for the day when God will grant the exiles victory over their oppressors. That's not to say they intend to carry out random acts of brutality – in fact they go on to seek the welfare of the oppressors' city, as instructed by God (Jeremiah 29 v 7; Daniel 6 v 1-3). But when a legitimate opportunity to destroy their enemies arrives, they take it with gladness (see Esther 9 v 1-17).

If that's the original meaning, how do we bridge the gap to our own time to get hold of the psalm's usefulness for "teaching, rebuking, correcting and training in righteousness"? Again, understanding the covenants is a vital part of the procedure. As we've seen throughout this book, while there's much in common throughout the valley of salvation history, some things change from one covenant field to the next. Sometimes the covenants have time-limited features, and that's definitely true in this case. As new covenant believers we no longer belong to a single nation state with territorial boundaries to defend; we're told military force shouldn't be used to promote God's kingdom (Matthew 26 v 52; John 18 v 36); and we're commanded to love our enemies and pray for those who persecute us (Matthew 5 v 44). So the psalm's original meaning will have different life applications for new covenant believers. As Christopher Ash puts it, we need to apply Old Testament texts "in ways appropriate to the new covenant".[78] This involves finding suitable points of contact between the earlier passage and our own new covenant times.

The violent final words of Psalm 137 have a lot in common with the second petition of the Lord's Prayer. It's a good point of contact between the psalm and the new covenant. Whenever we pray "your kingdom come" (Matthew 6 v 10), we're not only asking God to send Jesus back to rule over the world for ever, we're also calling on God to carry out his judgment on all those who live in rebellion against him, because the Bible teaches that the coming of Jesus' kingdom will coincide with the eternal destruction of God's enemies (Matthew 25 v 34, 41). So it's impossible to pray for the kingdom to come without simultaneously being in favour of God's punishment. Psalm 137 v 8-9 teaches new covenant believers that it's not wrong to cry out for the day when people in rebellion against God will be taken away from this world. In helping us to meditate on that future day, the psalm also makes us more eager to lead people to Jesus for his rescue.

The example above should demonstrate just how essential it is to be familiar with the covenants. Understanding a Bible passage requires hard thinking about its original covenant context, and how its meaning back then relates to the new covenant era. That means we need to figure out which covenant period each of the Old Testament books belongs to. The books of the Old Testament aren't in covenant order. Job, for example, probably lived during the time of the covenant with Noah.[79] Yet the book of Job appears in our Bibles immediately after Esther, which is set during the exile, three covenants and some 2000 years later! The table opposite seeks to put the Bible's books in their covenant order.

Once the covenant setting of a book has been established, it must be read with an eye on that particular covenant's terms of agreement. To return to the example of Job, we should be looking for indications that he trusts in the coming champion who'll redeem humanity; resists evil; and offers animal sacrifices. Those were the principal ways to express faith during the time of the covenant with Noah (bearing in mind that it incorporated the enduring features of the preceding covenants). So when we see Job offering sacrifices (1 v 5; 42 v 8), resisting temptation (1 v

Diagram 3: Books of the Old Testament in covenant order

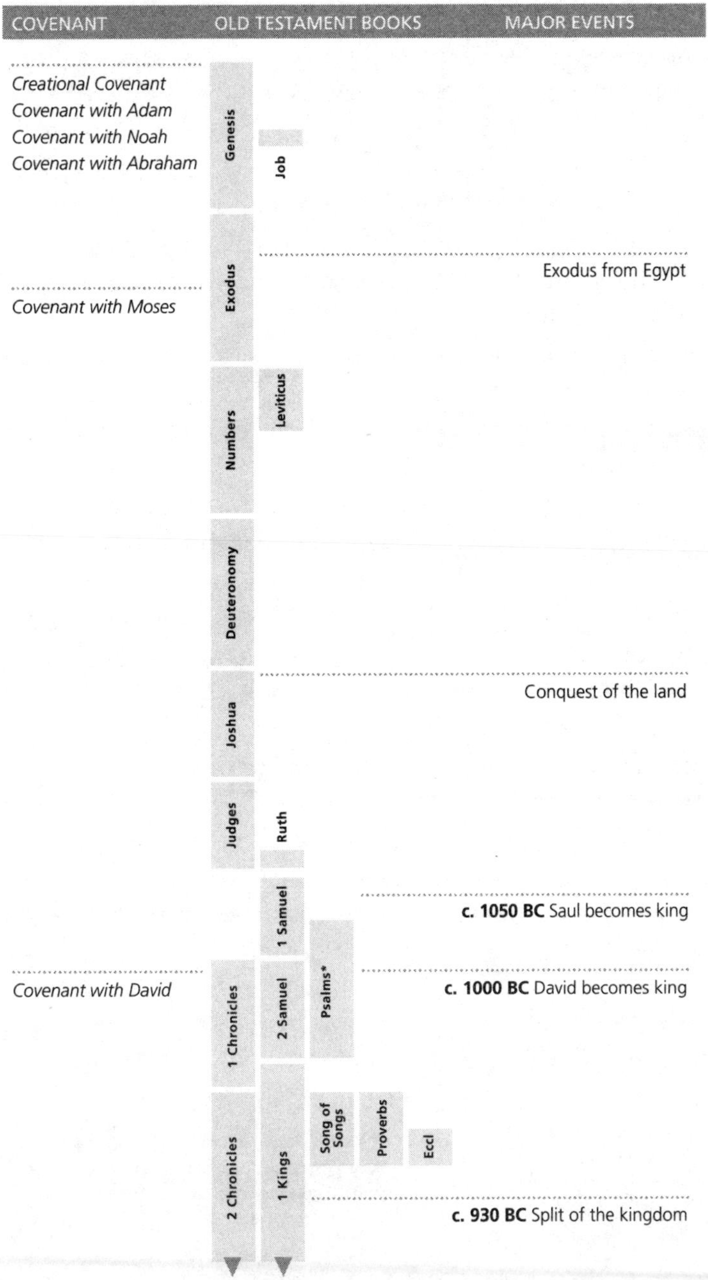

COVENANT	OLD TESTAMENT BOOKS	MAJOR EVENTS

Creational Covenant
Covenant with Adam
Covenant with Noah
Covenant with Abraham

Genesis

Job

Covenant with Moses

Exodus — Exodus from Egypt

Numbers — Leviticus

Deuteronomy

Joshua — Conquest of the land

Judges — Ruth

1 Samuel — **c. 1050 BC** Saul becomes king

Covenant with David

1 Chronicles — 2 Samuel — Psalms* — **c. 1000 BC** David becomes king

2 Chronicles — 1 Kings — Song of Songs — Proverbs — Eccl — **c. 930 BC** Split of the kingdom

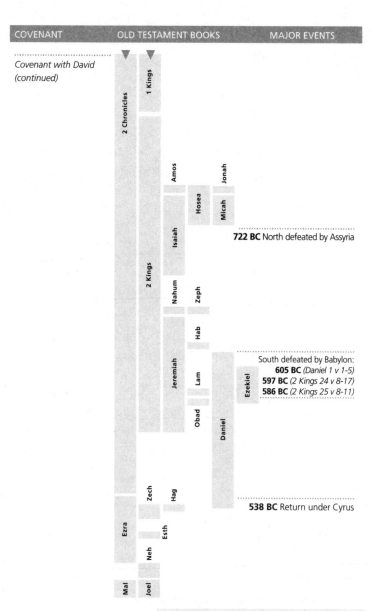

COVENANT	OLD TESTAMENT BOOKS	MAJOR EVENTS

*Covenant with David
(continued)*

2 Chronicles

1 Kings

2 Kings

Amos

Hosea

Jonah

Micah

Isaiah

722 BC North defeated by Assyria

Nahum

Zeph

Hab

Jeremiah

Lam

Obad

Ezekiel

Daniel

South defeated by Babylon:
605 BC *(Daniel 1 v 1-5)*
597 BC *(2 Kings 24 v 8-17)*
586 BC *(2 Kings 25 v 8-11)*

Zech

Hag

538 BC Return under Cyrus

Ezra

Esth

Neh

Mal

Joel

400 years of silence

New Covenant

* Psalms written throughout Israel's history
Books positioned by date of setting not authorship
See Appendix for notes on the dating of books

22) and trusting in the redeemer (19 v 25-27), we know he's holding on to covenant relationship with God despite his devastating afflictions. In this way the covenantal context helps us get a handle on the whole book.

The Old Testament contains many different kinds of literature: poetry, legal codes, proverbs, a love song, prophecies, historical narratives, biographies, military annals, prayers, dialogues, architectural plans, laments, and the strange but wonderful genre known as apocalypse. Despite this very wide variety of forms, the process of understanding and applying is the same throughout. First the meaning of the passage in its own covenant period has to be carefully ascertained, and then a legitimate point of contact needs to be found with our own new covenant situation. One fail-safe way of doing the latter is simply to ask what the passage reveals about God's character. Our triune God is unchanging (Malachi 3 v 6). So whatever is true of his character in Old Testament times is true of Father, Son and Spirit today.

No one denies that the history of salvation is made up of different epochs, each with its own code of conduct. But when Bible readers have overlooked the covenant principle, they've lost sight of the Bible's own way of drawing lines between those different periods. As O. Palmer Robertson says:

> The covenants are explicit scriptural indicators of divine initiatives that structure redemptive history.[80]

Not only are the covenants actually present in Scripture – thereby demanding an explanation of their role – they're also introduced at *times of transition* for God's people as momentous as creation itself. It's hard to see how the Bible could make their importance any clearer. The covenants reveal the changing terms of engagement between God and his people. They drive salvation history's progress.

Life lessons

- In the Bible the phrase "the Book of the Covenant" initially refers to a very short section of Exodus. We're told that Moses "took the Book of the Covenant and read it to the people" (Exodus 24 v 7). As the ESV Study Bible says, the phrase "most likely refers to both the Ten Commandments (20 v 1-21) and the commands and rules that follow (20 v 22 – 23 v 33)" – just four chapters of Scripture. Later in the Bible, Josiah assembles everyone in Jerusalem at the temple, where he reads "in their hearing all the words of the Book of the Covenant, which had been found in the temple of the Lord" (2 Kings 23 v 2). On this occasion the book being read is probably Deuteronomy (see Deuteronomy 31 v 24-26). So here the phrase "the Book of the Covenant" refers to a much larger portion of Scripture. It's perfectly appropriate to follow the Bible's example and continue widening the reach of the phrase to encompass all of God's written word. Peter Jensen explains the point like this: "The Bible as a whole may be called 'the Book of the Covenant', for in it the covenant of God is recorded, expounded and applied."[81] In chapter 2 we looked at the astonishing nature of God's *chesed*, his covenant love. Because the Bible is the Book of the Covenant, it's the longest and most detailed love letter in the world. So reading the Bible with an eye on the covenants is more than just the best approach for accurate interpretation. It helps us view the Bible in a relational way. **Every time we read the Bible, or hear it being read, or listen to faithful Bible teaching, we're in a position to deepen our covenant relationship with God.** That should put a spring in our step as we walk to church.

- It's surely not over-imaginative to say that in the course of eternity we'll have plenty of conversations with the prophet Ezekiel. Of course there won't be such a thing as embarrassment in God's perfect place, but you've got to wonder what the reaction will be when Ezekiel asks people: "So what did you make of my book?" Perhaps the conversation might go something like this:

"You mean you're really *the* Ezekiel, the prophet, the one who wrote that book in the Old Testament?"
"Yes, by the grace of God, that's me."
"Wow. Cool."
"Did you enjoy my book? What was your favourite part?"
"Oh. Good question."
"I'd be very interested to know."
"Well, it's hard to say."
"You must have had a favourite bit though."
"Well... it was all the word of God, wasn't it, so the whole of your book was equally great!"
"Hmm."
"If you're pushing me though, I'd say the part about the dead bones coming back to life. Chapter thirty-something, wasn't it? That was terrific."
"I'm so glad you liked it. It was one of my favourite parts

too. It was such a privilege to see that astonishing vision and then with God's help record it as Scripture. But what did you think of the passage earlier on about the glory departing from the temple?"

"To be honest, I'm not sure I ever read that chapter."

"Oh. [Long pause.] It was pretty significant. How about the parable of the two eagles and the vine?"

"I don't think I read that either."

"The lament for Israel's princes?"

"I guess it never came up in my Bible-reading notes."

"What did you make of the prophecy about the sword of the king of Babylon?"

"Ditto."

"Oh. How about..."

"Sorry Ezekiel, I should probably be on my way, but it's been great to meet you and I look forward to the next time our paths cross."

To put the point another way, if you yourself had written one of the Bible's sixty-six books, under the oversight of God Almighty, wouldn't you expect that God's people would treasure the contents of your book? So why is it that so many of the Bible's books are barely opened and only vaguely understood by modern western believers? We've lost our appetite for the Bible, even though it's the food we need for real life (Matthew 4 v 4). **God wants lovers of the word (Psalm 119 v 97), learners of the word (Deuteronomy 11 v 18), and livers of the word (James 1 v 22).** Jesus praised Mary for sitting at his feet, listening to what he said, while her sister Martha fussed over all kinds of unnecessaries: "Mary has chosen what is better, and it will not be taken away from her" (Luke 10 v 42). She is an example to follow.

One way to be Mary-like is to take on the exhilarating challenge of reading the Bible in a year. On the web there are all kinds of reading schemes designed to help with that, but they often rely on over-complicated lists of dates and passages. Some of them also require reading the New Testament and the Psalms twice over – hugely increasing the task. There's another approach that's easier to grasp and involves no double reading. The basic idea is to read two Old Testament chapters and one New Testament chapter a day. There are three twists:

- *On Sundays read an extra New Testament chapter.*
- *Include the Psalms in the New Testament reading track instead of the Old* (so once you've finished the New Testament, start reading one psalm a day and two on Sundays).
- *Don't include the book of Proverbs in either reading track.* Instead, since it has thirty-one chapters, pick a month with thirty-one days and read a chapter every night of that month (on top of your Bible reading earlier in the day).

You may find you get such a lot out of the experience that as soon as you've finished, you start over. "Let the wise listen and add to their learning" (Proverbs 1 v 5).

Let's make it our life's task to prize each of the sixty-six books that make up the Book of the Covenant. To love them, to learn them, and to live them, to the glory of God.

Acknowledgements

It's hard to exaggerate the esteem in which O. Palmer Robertson's book, *The Christ of the Covenants,* is held in evangelical academic circles. It's been in print since 1980, and is included on countless seminary reading lists. David Murray, Professor of Old Testament at Puritan Reformed Theological Seminary, goes as far as to say: "I'd never grasped the point of the Old Testament until I read *The Christ of the Covenants* by O. P. Robertson. When I read this, the lights went on."[82] For me, the experience of reading it was like having a thorn pulled from a paw. I already knew that salvation history was progressive, developing from one period to the next. But I wasn't sure how to identify the boundary lines between those periods. *The Christ of the Covenants* helped me by showing how each of the covenants gives rise to a new period of salvation history. As Robertson says (in a wonderful, thorn-pulling phrase), the covenants have "an epoch-making character."[83]

However, reading *The Christ of the Covenants* is a big ask. It's a long book that was clearly written with theological students and pastors in mind. Some years ago I studied it with a group of undergraduates at Durham University who needed quite a lot of help to get through it successfully. When I left Durham the following year, I felt it wouldn't be sensible to recommend Robertson's book to a similar group of students who were keen to read a Bible overview together. Instead I emailed them instalments of this book, which was designed to do the same job as *The Christ of the Covenants* in a briefer and more accessible way. I say all this simply to stress that I couldn't have written this book without *The*

Christ of the Covenants. I'm tremendously grateful for O. Palmer Robertson's careful exegesis, persuasive arguments and decisive conclusions.

The students who read *The Christ of the Covenants* with me were Nick Brake, Charlie Foster, Antonia Instone, Kate Merricks, Lucy Nicholl, Rosie O'Lone, Matt Pym, Ellie Quinn, Henry Swayne, James Taylor and Simon Tomkins. Happy memories of 36 The Avenue. The very patient and gracious students who had to put up with the first draft of this book the following year were Jonny Burgess, Pete Hicks, Lydia Mason, Bella Scott, James Taylor and Matt Taylor.

Robin Weekes's warm support of this book has been a great encouragement, and his many constructive comments were invaluable. Simon Tomkins read what I'd assumed was the final draft until his very helpful suggestions sent me back to my desk. I'm very grateful to Pete Hicks for creating the first of the book's three diagrams (later refined by André Parker), and it was kind of Sam Owen to provide the initial template for the third. I owe a great deal to Tim Thornborough from The Good Book Company for backing this project and making several nudges on the tiller that had a big influence on the way I wrote the book; and to Anne Woodcock, whose careful checking and insights improved the final product significantly.

I'm conscious that many thoughts that feel like my own are only in my head because of the ministry of others. The two names that particularly spring to mind are my former boss Paul Bolton, and Vaughan Roberts – whose preaching I had the huge privilege of sitting under for six years.

A final thank you goes to my very kind and loving parents, who had me to stay for what turned out to be an unexpectedly long wait for a visa, during which I worked on this book.

Endnotes

1   See Genesis 6 v 18; Genesis 15 v 18; Deuteronomy 5 v 2; 2 Samuel 7 (see 2 Samuel 23 v 5 and Psalm 89 v 3-4); and 1 Corinthians 11 v 25.

2   Jamie A. Grant and Alistair L. Wilson (eds), *The God of Covenant: Biblical, theological and contemporary perspectives* (Leicester: Apollos, 2005), p. 14. Their quotation from Scripture is a blend of Exodus 34 v 10 and 1 Kings 8 v 23.

3   I. Howard Marshall et al (eds), *New Bible Dictionary* (Leicester: Inter-Varsity Press, 1996). See the article "Covenant", by F.C. Fensham. This point would be more obvious to everyone if the Latin word *testamentum*, meaning both "testament" and "covenant", hadn't been wrongly translated "testament" instead of "covenant" in the early English Bibles. The title page for the first section of the Bible should read "Old Covenant", and the title page for the second, "New Covenant".

4   J.I. Packer, "On Covenant Theology", in *Celebrating the Saving Work of God: The Collected Shorter Writings of J.I. Packer, Volume 1* (Carlisle: Paternoster, 1998), 9-22, p. 13.

5   O. Palmer Robertson, *The Christ of the Covenants* (Phillipsburg, NJ: Presbyterian and Reformed, 1980), pp. 14-15.

6   There's a long-standing view that a covenant has also been made between the persons of the Trinity. But O. Palmer Robertson argues persuasively against this: "A sense of artificiality flavours the effort to structure in covenantal terms the mysteries of God's eternal counsels. Scripture simply does not say much on the pre-creation shape of the decrees of God. To speak concretely of an inter-trinitarian 'covenant' with terms and conditions between Father and Son mutually endorsed before the foundation of the world is to extend the bounds of scriptural evidence beyond propriety" (Robertson, p. 54).

7   Some theologians disagree. For example, Paul R. Williamson says "The biblical order is relationship, then covenant, rather than covenant, hence relationship" ("Covenant: the Beginning of a Biblical Idea", Reformed Theological Review, Vol. 65:1, April 2006, 1-14, p. 11). But taken as a whole, the biblical evidence makes it clear that covenants create relationships, instead of "sealing" or "formalising" them (as Williamson puts it). The marriage covenant, for example, creates a radically new relationship between a man and a woman. Through marriage a union exists that simply did not exist beforehand (Genesis 2 v 24). An even more important example is the new covenant, in Jesus' blood (Matthew 26 v 28; 1 Corinthians 11 v 25). Rather than sealing or formalising a pre-existing relationship, it makes relationship with God possible (see Ephesians 2 v 12-13).

8   The compressed definition borrows from Tim Keller's explanation of covenants: "God wants a covenant relationship with everybody ... A covenant relationship is a deep, intimate, emotional relationship with teeth in it" (from the first of two talks given at Oak Hill College titled "Preaching to the Heart", available online via oakhill.ac.uk/commentary/audio/).

9 Someone might say that "the blood of the eternal covenant" (Hebrews 13 v 20) refers only to the new covenant, not the seven covenants together. But elsewhere in Hebrews we're told, "Therefore he [Jesus] is the mediator of a new covenant, so that those who are called may receive the promised eternal inheritance, since a death has occurred that redeems them from the transgressions committed under the first covenant" (9 v 15, ESV). Here we find sins committed under the "first covenant" being paid for by blood shed under the new covenant (see also Romans 3 v 25-26). Through Jesus' blood all the covenants have become one.

10 Robertson, p. 42. The translation and (slightly adapted) observations are his.

11 Another passage proving this point is Zechariah's Song in Luke chapter 1. In verses 72-73 Zechariah says that God has remembered his "holy covenant", which he describes as "the oath he swore to our father Abraham". Verses 69-70 similarly demonstrate the enduring significance of the covenant with David. Yet it needs to be underlined that former covenants don't live on in their own right as valid ways of relating to God. Hebrews 8 v 13 rules that out: "By calling this covenant 'new', he has made the first one obsolete; and what is obsolete and ageing will soon disappear." God stays true to previous covenants by incorporating their most vital components into later covenants. This incorporation principle can be clearly seen in Hebrews, where the covenant with Moses is called "the first covenant' (9 v 18-20). This description would contradict 6 v 13-18, which upholds the ongoing significance of the earlier covenant with Abraham, unless both covenants are being rolled together and treated as one.

12 David Adams Leeming, *Creation Myths of the World* (Santa Barbara: ABC-CLIO, 2010), p. 324; Barbara C. Sproul, *Creation Myths Around the World* (New York: HarperCollins, 1991), pp. 44, 253.

13 Hosea 6 v 7 is not universally accepted as evidence for a creational covenant. Paul Williamson, for example, lists several alternative ways to understand the verse (Williamson, p. 3). But the only plausible option on his list that doesn't require a change to the Hebrew text is to replace "Adam" with "man" or "mankind". As O. Palmer Robertson explains, that would also indicate the existence of a creational covenant (Robertson, pp. 22-24). Another relevant verse is Isaiah 24 v 5: "The earth is defiled by its people; they have disobeyed the laws, violated the statutes and broken the everlasting covenant." Which covenant could be in view if not the creational covenant? It calls for the beneficial subduing of the world, but Isaiah says humanity has instead "defiled" the earth. It's also important to note that the covenant with David (2 Samuel 7) is only described as a covenant long after the event (2 Samuel 23 v 5). This proves beyond question that a covenant can be agreed without the term itself being used. The Bible has a tendency not to label everything along the way. The seventh day of creation week, for example, is not called the Sabbath in Genesis 2 v 3, but is described as the Sabbath in Exodus 20 v 11. Eve's tempter is not described as Satan in the creation account itself. And the champion of Genesis 3 v 15 is not described as the Messiah. We don't need those terms to be present to identify the Sabbath, Satan, and the Messiah correctly.

14 The covenant made at the time of creation has traditionally been called the "covenant of works", in contrast with the "covenant of grace" established after the fall. But the helpfulness of this title is questionable. It detracts from the grace received by

mankind in Eden. As O. Palmer Robertson says: "The totality of God's relationship with man is a matter of grace" (Robertson, p. 56).

15 Christopher Ash, *Marriage: Sex in the service of God* (Leicester: IVP, 2003), p. 114.

16 Sharon James, *God's Design for Women: Biblical Womanhood for Today* (Darlington: Evangelical Press, 2002), p. 78.

17 There is an interesting discussion of this passage in Robert Alter, T*he Art of Biblical Narrative* (New York: Basic Books, 1981), pp. 31-32. Alter draws a comparison with Plato's *The Symposium,* in which lovers seek to "recapture that impossible primal unity."

18 Thomas R. Schreiner gives a very helpful survey of all the biblical material in "A New Testament Perspective on Homosexuality", *Themelios* 31/3, pp. 62-75. Googling the title should bring up the article online.

19 Divorce and remarriage seem to be permitted in the New Testament in cases where the original union has already been broken through adultery, or desertion by an unbelieving spouse. See Matthew 19 v 9 and 1 Corinthians 7 v 15. Some Christians argue that there are no grounds for remarriage in the New Testament.

20 Clyde Ervine, "Single in the Church: Eunuchs in the Kingdom", *Churchman*, Autumn 2005, 217-232, p. 221. The article focuses on Matthew 19 v 3-12. It's available on the web – just google the title.

21 John Stott argues convincingly that 1 Thessalonians 4 v 4 means: "Each of you should learn to acquire a wife" (NIV margin) rather than "Each of you should learn to control his own body" (NIV main text). See John R.W. Stott, *The Message of Thessalonians* (Leicester: IVP, 1991), pp. 82ff. Paul's advice in verse 4 follows his command: "You should avoid sexual immorality" (verse 3).

22 The gifts referred to by Paul in 1 Corinthians 7 v 7 are generally understood to be the gifts of marriage and singleness, with the latter usually taken to be a special ability to cope well with celibacy (see the comments in the *ESV Study Bible* [Wheaton: Crossway, 2008]). Some argue, however, that the gift of singleness is simply the state of being single (see for example Albert Y. Hsu, *Singles at the Crossroads* [Downers Grove: InterVarsity Press, 1997], pp. 58-59). But that doesn't seem to fit Paul's argument in 1 Corinthians 7 v 1-7. He begins by advising people to get married to avoid sexual immorality (v 1-2). Then in verse 7 he says that he wishes everyone could be single like him. This creates a contradiction, because we're told in 11 v 1 to follow Paul's example. The contradiction is only resolved if the gift of singleness that Paul mentions later in 7 v 7 refers to a God-given suitability for lifelong singleness that he knows most people lack – hence the advice in verse 2. There's a parallel passage in Matthew 19 that seems to confirm this interpretation. When the disciples say, "It is better not to marry" (v 10), Jesus replies, "Not everyone can accept this word, but only those to whom it has been given." It's clear from verse 12 that this gifted category is not made up of all singles everywhere, and so the gift of singleness cannot be the state of being single.

23 It's sometimes said that the Sabbath was an illustration of the rest that has now been provided by Jesus. According to this argument the Sabbath belongs in the "shadow" category (that is, things awaiting fulfilment in Jesus), which at first glance seems to be confirmed by Colossians 2 v 16-17. But verse 16 literally says "sabbaths" rather than "the Sabbath", and the word "sabbath" can refer to festival rest days (see

Leviticus 23 v 32). It's likely that Paul has these in mind, given the plural form, and the respect he shows elsewhere for the weekly day of religious observance (Acts 20 v 7; 1 Corinthians 16 v 2). Although Jesus does of course provide rest (Matthew 11 v 28-30), believers don't yet enjoy rest in every sense (see Hebrews 4 v 9-11; Revelation 14 v 13), and so we still need the Sabbath. Another argument sometimes put forward against the ongoing need for Sabbath observance is based on Romans 14 v 5-6. It's said that in these verses Paul makes Sabbath observance an optional matter to be settled by the individual conscience. But as with Colossians 2 v 16-17, it's highly questionable whether the weekly Sabbath is in view. If Paul is taking Sabbath observance for granted as a creational ordinance, then the days at issue in Romans 14 v 5-6 would be (as in Colossians 2 v 16-17) Jewish festivals, festival rest days, and new moon celebrations.

24 J.C. Ryle, *Knots Untied* (London: C.J. Thynne, 1902), p. 302.

25 Seventh Day Adventists and many Jewish believers in Jesus regard Saturday as the continuing day of the Sabbath.

26 Jesus gives an example of Sabbath flexibility when he teaches that if people have "an ox that falls into a well" on the Sabbath, they should haul it out (Luke 14 v 5) – thereby permitting emergency work. He also points out that ministry duties may cause people to "desecrate the day" while remaining "innocent" (Matthew 12 v 5). And he insists that it's right to heal on the Sabbath (Mark 3 v 3-5).

27 Robert Isaac Wilberforce and Samuel Wilberforce, *The Life of William Wilberforce* (London: John Murray, 1838), vol. 3, p. 3. The date of the journal entry is February 8th, 1801.

28 Revelation 2 v 7 says: "To him who overcomes, I will give the right to eat from the tree of life, which is in the paradise of God." The presence of the tree of life in the world to come is a clear echo of Eden. And the Greek word translated "paradise" could just as easily be translated "garden". It's the word used for the Garden of Eden in the Septuagint (a Greek version of the Old Testament well known to the writers of the New Testament).

29 Micah 7 v 17 alludes to the curse on the snake (Genesis 3 v 14-15) when describing a regular snake. Romans 16 v 20 alludes to the same curse when prophesying Satan's final destruction. This double application of the curse only makes sense if both the animal and Satan were involved in the tempting of Eve. Further proof of Satan's involvement is found in Revelation 12 v 9, which identifies Satan as "that ancient serpent". And Jesus almost definitely has the tempting of Eve in mind when he says: "The devil … was a murderer from the beginning, not holding to the truth, for there is no truth in him" (John 8 v 44).

30 The slaying of animals (3 v 21) can be viewed as a kind of covenant opening ceremony (see chapter 1 of this book). Adam and Eve would have seen death for the first time at that point, bringing home the consequences of covenant breaking. The lack of a similar blood-shedding ceremony to mark the opening of the creational covenant can be explained by the absence of death before the fall.

31 C.H. Spurgeon, "Christ the Conqueror of Satan", a sermon preached on November 26th 1876, (available via spurgeon.org).

32 The key to working out whether the Hebrew word *zera* (= offspring) refers to a group

or an individual is to see whether the words connected to it are plural or singular in form. In Battle #2 there are no connected words to guide us. In Battle #3 the words connected to *zera* are singular. So assuming it's right to say that Battle #2 is fought between two groups, that would mean *zera* initially refers to a group, and then, via the pronoun *hu* (= he), to just one representative individual in Battle #3. That's by no means unlikely, because precisely the same kind of switch happens in the Hebrew of Genesis 22 v 17 (as captured by the ESV). See James Hamilton, "The Skull Crushing Seed of the Woman: Inner-Biblical Interpretation of Genesis 3:15", *Southern Baptist Journal of Theology 10.2* (2006), 30–54, p. 32. The article is available online (via beginningwithmoses.org). There's another reason why the combatant in Battle #3 is a single individual. Between Battles #2 and #3 the enemy narrows from Satan's offspring back to Satan himself, and there needs to be a similar narrowing on the other side to keep the match-ups equivalent.

33 The Hebrew words translated "desire" and "rule over" are also found in Genesis 4 v 7, where God says to Cain: "Sin is crouching at the door. Its desire is for you, but you must rule over it" (ESV). In view of that parallel, God is telling Eve in Genesis 3 v 16 that her natural impulse will be to control her husband.

34 The common translation: "I have acquired a man with the LORD" (i.e. with the help of the LORD), treats the Hebrew particle *'et* as a preposition meaning "with", rather than treating it as the (untranslatable) mark of a direct object. It's true that *'et* can have either meaning, and verses such as Genesis 21 v 20; 39 v 2, 21 are cited as parallels for "with". But in those verses *'et* has to mean "with" because of the presence of the verb "to be", e.g.: "the LORD was with him" (Genesis 39 v 21). That verb isn't used in Genesis 4 v 1. What's more, both of the other names in Genesis 4 v 1 – Eve and Cain – are preceded by *'et*, used to denote the accusative rather than to mean "with".

35 James P. Boyce, *Abstract of Systematic Theology* (1887), ch. 25 (available online via founders.org).

36 Adam calls his wife "Eve", which in Hebrew sounds like the verb meaning "to live". We're told this is "because she would become the mother of all the living" (Genesis 3 v 20). It's striking that she receives this name straight after God has said that she and Adam will die because of their disobedience (3 v 19). It suggests there's a spiritual meaning to Eve's name: she truly is the mother of all the living because in Battle #2 of Genesis 3 v 15 her "offspring" are those who follow her example and fight against Satan. Because of their saviour's victory they will be granted permission to eat from the tree of life (Revelation 2 v 7).

37 The New Testament supports the view that Abel's sacrifice was superior because of the presence of atoning blood. Hebrews 11 v 4 says: "By faith Abel offered God a better sacrifice than Cain did." This comes shortly after the author has said: "Without the shedding of blood there is no forgiveness" (9 v 22). Animal sacrifices were offered not only by Abel but also by Noah, Abraham and others, long before the first full explanation in the Bible of the role of blood in atonement (Leviticus 17 v 11). There's no reason to assume that they didn't understand the significance of what they were doing, simply because of the Bible's delay in spelling out the explanation. The Puritan theologian John Owen is quick to credit Abel with full comprehension of his actions: 'he offered a bloody sacrifice, in faith of the future propitiation by the Seed of the woman' *An Exposition of the Epistle to the Hebrews*, vol. 7 (from *The Works of John Owen, vol.*

24 [Edinburgh: T. & T. Clark, 1862], p. 45, accessed via openlibrary.org).

38 Sadly, by March 2011 all twenty had perished and the species was extinct (Justin Gilligan, "Island on the Edge", ECOS 159).

39 John Calvin, *Commentary on Genesis*, chapter 9, (accessed via ccel.org).

40 *The Times*, August 5th 2011, p. 2.

41 The apostles banned the eating of blood in their letter to the Gentile churches (Acts 15 v 23-29), which means the prohibition continued for a limited period in new covenant times. Since animal sacrifices had obviously lost their significance following the death of Jesus, why did the apostles want people to avoid eating blood? Their ban was issued at a time when some false teachers were calling for total conformity by Gentiles to the Law of Moses (Acts 15 v 1). The apostles rejected that message (Acts 15 v 24), but they did make certain requirements based on the Law of Moses (15 v 21), including the ban on eating blood. That was probably because it was important for all believers to respect certain well-known Jewish customs while the message of the Jewish Messiah was first being announced to synagogues throughout the nations. It was a point in salvation history when it was necessary for everyone to become "like a Jew, to win the Jews" (1 Corinthians 9 v 20) in the particular ways chosen by the apostles. But as Romans 14 v 14 indicates, the ban was not permanent. In Scotland what's known as black pudding is largely made of blood. It's sometimes sold covered in batter and deep-fried. There are no theological reasons to avoid it.

42 The Greek could also be translated "found out" or "exposed". Translations that have "burnt up" are following a variant reading found in later, less reliable manuscripts (see the excellent note on 2 Peter 3 v 10 in the *ESV Study Bible*). The NIV's translation of 3 v 11, "Since everything will be destroyed in this way…", is regrettable. The Greek says "all these things" (which could refer simply to "the heavens" and "the elements" of verse 10) rather than "everything". It can't be right to think that "everything will be destroyed", since verse 10 says that the earth will be "laid bare", and Romans 8 v 19-21 teaches that this earth has a future.

43 Robert Murray M'Cheyne, "Our Duty to Israel", a sermon preached on November 17th 1839 (available via mcheyne.info).

44 As Hebrews 11 v 13-16 makes clear, the land promised to Abraham and his descendants will be granted to them at the time of their resurrection. Any possession of the land by Abraham's descendants beforehand should be understood as a partial fulfilment of that promise: a sign of God's faithfulness and token – for covenant believers – of more to follow in the world to come. We must be careful not to misread Old Testament prophecies about a return to the land as references to modern Israel. Those prophecies refer either to the return from Babylon in 538 BC or to the ultimate fulfilment of God's promise to Abraham. In the New Testament, however, Matthew 10 v 23 seems to indicate that Jesus expects the state of Israel to be in existence at the time of his return. For many centuries between 70 AD and 1948 that appeared impossible, but "nothing is impossible with God" (Luke 1 v 37).

45 Robertson, p. 146.

46 Psalm 25 confirms that pursuing blamelessness in God's sight (verses 4-5) is part of keeping "the demands of his covenant" (verse 10); yet this isn't understood as attaining sinless perfection (see verses 11, 18). On the other hand Numbers 15 v 30-31 demonstrates the consequences of refusing to pursue blamelessness: "But anyone who sins defiantly, whether native-born or alien, blasphemes the LORD, and that person must be cut off from his people. Because he has despised the LORD's word and broken his commands, that person must surely be cut off; his guilt remains on him." Such a person no longer receives any of the covenant's benefits – see verses 32-36. See also Deuteronomy 29 v 18-21; Joshua 23 v 16; and 2 Kings 17 v 15.

47 See Leviticus 19 v 23, where "forbidden" is literally "uncircumcised" and is a synonym for "unclean"; and John 7 v 22-23, where careful study of Jesus' argument shows that circumcision was thought of as a small-scale healing. The foreskin had to be removed to make a child well.

48 Michael Horton, *Introducing Covenant Theology* (Grand Rapids: Baker Books, 2009), p. 146.

49 To speak of a spiritual Israel does not mean that Jewish believers in Jesus lose their distinctive Jewish identity (see Acts 21 v 39; Romans 11 v 1; Colossians 4 v 10-11). Nor does it mean that racial Israel – that is, the worldwide Jewish population – has lost its special place in God's heart and purposes (see Romans 11 v 28-31).

50 Dale Ralph Davis, *1 Samuel: Looking on the Heart* (Fearn: Christian Focus, 2000), p. 97.

51 I'm grateful to Mervyn Eloff for a talk on Exodus 2 that transformed my understanding of the passage.

52 Cited in Joseph Strutt, *The Sports and Pastimes of the People of England* (London: Methuen, 1903), p. 96.

53 Some commentators compare the covenant with Moses unfavourably with the Abrahamic covenant (see Horton, p. 97). According to this view, the covenant with Abraham is one of the "unconditional covenants that announce a divine promise", while the covenant with Moses is one of the "conditional covenants that impose obligations" (p. 36), and therefore "there is no mercy in the Sinaitic covenant itself" (p. 50). But this interpretation overlooks the many elements of promise in the covenant with Moses, such as God's gracious presence in the tabernacle – which is a first step towards full reunion – and the merciful sacrificial system, which is a "shadow of the good things that are coming" (Hebrews 10 v 1). It also neglects the legal element in the covenant with Abraham: "The LORD appeared to Abram and said to him, 'I am God Almighty; walk before me, and be blameless, *that I may make* my covenant between me and you'" (Genesis 17 v 1-2, ESV). This demonstrates plainly that the covenant with Abraham is conditional on his pursuit of blameless obedience (see also Genesis 26 v 4-5). The same kind of conditionality is easy to find in another "promise covenant": the new covenant (see Matthew 6 v 14-15, Romans 8 v 13 or Hebrews 12 v 14). It's true that Paul makes harsh comments about the Law of Moses, but in context these always refer to the mistaken "works salvation" view of the law that was common at the time. When, for example, he says, "The law is not based on faith" (Galatians 3 v 12), he's referring to the distorted understanding of the law held by the so-called Judaizers, who "rely on observing the law" (3 v 10), "are trying to be justified by law" (5 v 4), and consider the cross offensive (5 v 11). Their misreading of the law leaves no room for the faith that saves (3 v 11). Paul's negative descriptions of the old covenant as "the ministry of death" and "the ministry of condemnation" (2 Corinthians 3 v 7, 9, ESV) also come in the context of opposing Judaizers (3 v 1; 11 v 22). The law condemns to death those who *mistakenly* seek "legalistic righteousness" (Philippians 3 v 6, see also Romans 9 v 31-32). The Judaizers misinterpreted the covenant with Moses. Surely it can't be right to read Scripture as they did.

54 Robertson, p. 175.

55 For example, the covenant with Noah doesn't mention the promise of the redeemer.

56 It's obviously different for Jewish believers in Jesus, since their culture largely comes from the Law of Moses. Jewish believers often keep some or all of the cultural parts of the law, following in the footsteps of the first believers in Jerusalem (Acts 21 v 20-26). This is also an important aspect of Jewish outreach (1 Corinthians 9 v 20; Acts 16 v 1-3). But Peter and Paul, though Jewish themselves, were willing to drop Jewish customs when among Gentiles (see Galatians 2 v 14 and 1 Corinthians 9 v 21). This shows that obeying the cultural side of the law is optional for Jewish believers.

57 The Ten Commandments are all restated in the New Testament. So they have ongoing force even for those who argue that Old Testament laws need to be reaffirmed in the New to apply today. See these verses, which follow the original order of the commandments: Matthew 4 v 10; Galatians 5 v 20; 1 Timothy 6 v 1; Matthew 24 v 20; Matthew 19 v 18-19; Luke 12 v 15. The third commandment is more closely reflected in 1 Timothy 6 v 1 than might at first be apparent. The familiar English version of Exodus 20 v 7 – "you shall not take the LORD's name in vain" – translates a Hebrew verb that literally means "lift up" or "bear": the command therefore calls for appropriate behaviour in every respect by the bearers of God's name, not just the avoidance of blasphemy. Paul is warning Christian slaves that disrespectful behaviour towards their masters will lead to the slandering of the name they bear. An excellent book on the Ten Commandments is the well-named *Love Rules: The Ten Commandments for the 21st Century* (Edinburgh: Banner of Truth, 2007).

58 It's not clear why David leaves the tabernacle at Gibeon, where it's used as a separate centre of worship (1 Chronicles 16 v 39-40; 2 Chronicles 1 v 3-6). But in the biblical accounts this doesn't detract from the national renewal resulting from the coming of the ark to Jerusalem (1 Chronicles 15 v 28). In Jerusalem David pitches a new tent around the ark (1 Chronicles 16 v 1).

59 "After 217 years, the last Dr Maurice of Marlborough hangs up his stethoscope", *Daily Telegraph*, August 27th, 2009.

60 It's possible to get confused about the Bible's attitude to the kingship, because in 1 Samuel 12 v 17-18 the Israelites are punished for asking for a king. But that's because they ask with rebellious motives (8 v 7). The prophecy in Genesis 49 v 10 shows that kings were always on the agenda for Israel; the Law of Moses caters for future kings (Deuteronomy 17 v 14-20); and the comments of the narrator of Judges quoted above demonstrate a high regard for the king's role. God does, however, reveal in advance the terrible harm that ungodly kings will cause (1 Samuel 8 v 17-18).

61 The word "Messiah" is the English version of the Hebrew word *mashiach*. It means "anointed one" and was originally simply an alternative way of saying "king" (see 1 Samuel 12 v 3). But over time *mashiach*, and its Greek equivalent *christos*, came to be used with specific reference to the promised eternal King (see Psalm 2 v 2; Daniel

9 v 26; John 4 v 25; John 12 v 34).

62 Peter Godwin, *When a Crocodile Eats the Sun* (New York: Back Bay, 2008), p. 48.

63 Sam Harris, for example, the author of *Letter to a Christian Nation*, has said: "Faith is the license that religious people give one another to keep believing when reasons fail, to keep believing in the absence of evidence ... The problem with faith is that it really is a conversation stopper ... it's a reason why you do not have to give reasons for what you believe" ("The View from the End of the World", a Long Now Foundation seminar, December 2005).

64 In addition to the prophecies in Isaiah discussed above, Old Testament messianic prophecies include (among many others) the Messiah's tribe – Genesis 49 v 10; the timing of his arrival – Daniel 2 v 44; the locations of his birth – Micah 5 v 2, and death – Daniel 9 v 25-26; and his rejection by the nation's leaders – Psalm 118 v 22. For further reading see Michael L. Brown, *Answering Jewish Objections to Jesus Volume 3: Messianic Prophecy Objections* (Grand Rapids: Baker Books, 2003).

65 The different ways in which people can get involved are explored in John Dickson's very wise book *Promoting the Gospel: A practical guide to the biblical art of sharing your faith* (Sydney: Blue Bottle Books, 2005).

66 When the prophet Daniel prays in exile for God to "look with favour" on Jerusalem (Daniel 9 v 17-18), the angel Gabriel answers by discussing the coming of the Messiah (9 v 25-26), not the return that was about to take place under Cyrus. In the New Testament Simeon is said to be "waiting for the consolation of Israel" (Luke 2 v 25), and Anna is among those "looking forward to the redemption of Jerusalem" (2 v 38). Note the future focus. They pin their hopes on the baby brought to the temple by Mary and Joseph (Luke 2 v 26-32, 38). See also Luke 1 v 68-75.

67 "Her Life Was Turned Upside Down", *BBC Online*, June 14th, 2005; "My Life Changed in a Second", *BBC Online*, September 30th, 2005.

68 This covenant clause results in a change of emphasis concerning the Spirit's work as the Old Testament gives way to the New. The former emphasises his work in particular people for particular purposes at particular times (see for example Numbers 11 v 16-29; Judges 14 v 6; 1 Samuel 10 v 5-11). The New Testament, however, emphasises the Spirit's work in all God's people (Romans 8 v 9; 1 Corinthians 12 v 7; 2 Corinthians 1 v 22; Ephesians 1 v 13-14). While the Spirit must have been at work in Old Testament times opening blind eyes and keeping people in God's service, there seems to be no promise of permanent indwelling. David's prayer, "Do not ... take your Holy Spirit from me" (Psalm 51 v 11) is therefore appropriate for an old covenant believer but inappropriate for new covenant use.

69 The image of the natural and wild branches in Romans 11 v 16-24 is reflected in C. S. Lewis's comment, "In a sense the converted Jew is the only normal human being in the world. To him, in the first instance, the promises were made, and he has availed himself of them. He calls Abraham his father by hereditary right as well as by divine courtesy ... Everyone else is, from one point of view, a special case" (from his foreword to *Smoke on the Mountain* by Joy Davidman [Philadelphia: Westminster Press, 1953], pp. 7-8).

70 Elsewhere there are other examples of terminology formerly used of the nation of Israel being applied to all new covenant believers. Paul insists that the Philippians,

including uncircumcised Gentiles, are "the circumcision" (Philippians 3 v 3). And Peter lifts terms from Exodus 19 when he describes mainly Gentile believers as "a chosen people, a royal priesthood, a holy nation, a people belonging to God" (1 Peter 2 v 9).

71 For example, when Paul says, "And in this way all Israel will be saved" (Romans 11 v 26, ESV), does he mean racial Israel or the newly-formed body of believers that is also known as Israel?

72 Ray Galea, *God is Enough* (Kingsford: Matthias Media, 2010), p. 74.

73 It's often pointed out that the criminal on the cross next to Jesus was saved without being baptised. That observation is true and helpful. Although Ananias presents baptism as the way in, it's by no means the only way of expressing saving faith. But that doesn't mean that baptism is optional. If the criminal had somehow survived crucifixion, he would have needed to be baptised in order to submit to the command of his King (Matthew 28 v 19).

74 John Piper, "Charles Spurgeon: Preaching through Adversity", a biographical address available via desiringgod.org.

75 John R. W. Stott, *The Message of Galatians* (London: IVP, 1968), p. 179.

76 The sixteenth century reformer and martyr John Hooper expresses the point like this: "The justification of man [comes] only by faith in Jesus Christ, and not by the merit of any man's good works, albeit that good works do necessarily follow justification, the which before justification are of no value or estimation before God." J.C. Ryle, *Five English Reformers* (1890, reprint ed., Edinburgh: Banner of Truth, 1981), pp. 63-64.

77 The kingdom spoken of by the disciples in Acts 1 v 6 is understood differently by Premillennialists. According to Premillennialism, Jesus will reign for a thousand years over the state of Israel, after the rapture of believers but before the start of the new creation. Premillennialists see Acts 1 v 6 as a reference to *that* kingdom (see for example John McArthur, *The McArthur New Testament Commentary: Acts 1-12* [Chicago: Moody, 1994], p. 20). Yet seven different New Testament writers say that we're currently in the *last* days (see Acts 2 v 17; 2 Timothy 3 v 1; Hebrews 1 v 2; James 5 v 3; 1 Peter 1 v 20; 1 John 2 v 18; Jude 18-19). What's more, Paul says that new covenant believers are the people "on whom the fulfilment of the ages has come" (1 Corinthians 10 v 11). It's hard to make sense of this language of finality and fulfilment if a thousand-year period is still to come, between Jesus' return and the Day of Judgment. John's vision of the millennium (Revelation 20 v 1-10), like other visions in Revelation, contains numerous symbols – such as the key, the chain, the dragon, and the beast. These symbols are not meant to be taken literally. The millennium itself can also be regarded as a figurative way of expressing spiritual truth about our own age. To insist that it must be taken literally is to misunderstand the nature of the apocalypse genre.

78 Christopher Ash, *The Priority of Preaching* (Fearn: Christian Focus, 2009), p. 101.

79 There is no mention of Israel, which suggests that Job lived before the covenant with Abraham. And by Job's time the world's population had evidently been divided into different ethnic groups (see Job 1 v 15, 17), which happened after the flood. Scholars disagree on when Job was written, but since it is *set* during the time of the covenant with Noah, it's that covenant which is most relevant to our understanding of the book.

80 Robertson, p. 227.

81 Peter Jensen, *The Revelation of God* (Downers Grove: IVP, 2002), p. 81. The point is also explored in David Gibson's article "The God of Promise: Christian Scripture as Covenantal Revelation" (available via theologynetwork.org). Gibson points out the equivalence between the phrases, "when the old covenant is read" and "when Moses is read" in 2 Corinthians 3 v 14-15, which shows that Paul views the entire Torah as a single covenant document. Given the additional examples discussed above, it therefore seems clear that within the Bible any portion of Scripture, no matter how short or long, can be described in covenantal terms. Tim Keller speaks about the covenantal nature of the Bible in the first of his talks titled "Preaching to the Heart" (available via oakhill.ac.uk/commentary/audio/). He says: "The Bible is a covenant document, that is to say I believe the Bible is an invitation from our covenant Lord to serve him in love and fidelity ... everything that the Bible reveals, everything in the document ... is revealed not just to be known but to be obeyed ... there's no speculative theological reflection ... the only things that God puts in the Bible are things that are germane to covenant fidelity and service. It's a covenant document."

82 David Murray, "Top 20 most influential books in my life", June 21st 2011 (available via headhearthand.org/blog/).

83 Robertson, p. 27.

Appendix

Notes on the date of OT Books (setting, not authorship)

Genesis records the beginning of salvation history. **Job** doesn't mention Israel, which suggests it is set before the covenant with Abraham (Genesis 12 v 1-7). **Exodus**, which ends with the construction of the tabernacle, precedes **Leviticus** and **Numbers**, both of which refer to the tabernacle. The first section of Numbers shares the same Sinai setting as Leviticus (Leviticus 27 v 34; Numbers 1 v 1; 10 v 12-13); the rest of Numbers post-dates Leviticus and pre-dates **Deuteronomy** (compare Numbers 33 v 38 with Deuteronomy 1 v 3). Deuteronomy, **Joshua**, and **Judges** are sequential (see Joshua 1 v 1; Judges 1 v 1).

The events of **Ruth** happen shortly before those of **1 Samuel** – or possibly coincide with the period of 1 Samuel chapters 1-3 (David was an adult at the time of Samuel's death [1 Samuel 25 v 1], which puts David's great-grandfather Boaz [Ruth 4 v 21-22] in the generation before Samuel). 1 Samuel must post-date Judges as Samuel isn't mentioned in Judges despite being "judge over Israel all the days of his life" (1 Samuel 7 v 15). **1 & 2 Kings** follow on from **2 Samuel** and continue to the Babylonian exile. **1 Chronicles** begins with a largely genealogical survey of Israelite history from Adam to the returnees in 538 BC and beyond (see 1 Chronicles 1 v 1; 9 v 1-34); its setting from chapter 10 onwards is the same as 2 Samuel and the start of 1 Kings. **2 Chronicles** covers the same period as 1 and 2 Kings but extends beyond them to the end of the Babylonian exile (2 Chronicles 36 v 23). The **Psalms** are set throughout Israel's history, from the time of Moses (Psalm 90) to the Babylonian exile (Psalm 137) and possibly beyond (Psalm 126); but the book is particularly associated with King David.

Proverbs, Song of Songs, and **Ecclesiastes** are all associated with King Solomon (see Proverbs 1 v 1; Song of Songs 1 v 1; Ecclesiastes 1 v 1, 12 [cf. 2 Chronicles 9 v 30], 16; 2 v 9 [cf. 1 Kings 3 v 12]; 12 v 9). **Jonah** is set in the first half of the eighth century BC, during the reign of Jeroboam II (see 2 Kings 14 v 25); **Amos** is also set during Jeroboam's reign (Amos 1 v 1). The setting of **Isaiah** stretches from the year King Uzziah died (Isaiah 6 v 1), c. 740 BC, to 681 BC (37 v 38). Both **Hosea** and **Micah** are set in the decades leading up to the 722 BC defeat of Israel (see Hosea 13 v 16; Micah 6 v 16), but the period in view in Hosea begins one reign earlier (see Hosea 1 v 1; Micah 1 v 1). **Zephaniah** is set in the second half of the seventh century BC during the reign of Josiah (Zephaniah 1 v 1), before the 612 BC destruction of Nineveh (see 2 v 13). **Nahum** also predates the destruction of Nineveh (Nahum 1 v 1).

Jeremiah begins c. 627 BC, in the thirteenth year of Josiah (Jeremiah 1 v 2), and finishes after 560 BC (52 v 31-34). **Habakkuk** is set shortly before the first Babylonian invasion in 605 BC (Habakkuk 1 v 6). **Daniel** covers seventy years from 605 BC (Daniel 1 v 1) to 536 BC (10 v 1), shortly after the return of the Israelites to Jerusalem. The setting of **Ezekiel** is a twenty-two year period from 593 BC (Ezekiel 1 v 2) to 571 BC (29 v 17). **Lamentations** is set during the destruction of Jerusalem in 586 BC (Lamentations 1 v 1; 2 v 21; chapter 4); and **Obadiah** shortly afterwards (Obadiah 12-15).

The whole of **Haggai** is set in 520 BC (Haggai 1 v 1; 2 v 10). **Zechariah** begins in the same year (Zechariah 1 v 1), and the prophecies it records continue for a further two years (7 v 1). The events of **Esther** take place under King Xerxes (Esther 1 v 1), who ruled the Persian Empire from 486-465 BC. The first half of Ezra deals with the period from the return in 538 BC to the first Passover in the second temple in 515 BC (Ezra 1 v 1 – 6 v 22); **Ezra** then switches to a later generation's return in 458 BC (7 v 1, 8). **Nehemiah** begins in 445 BC (see Nehemiah 1 v 1, 2 v 1) and finishes some time after 433 BC (13 v 6-7). **Malachi** post-dates Zechariah, because the second temple has already been built (Malachi 1 v 10). **Joel** must also be set after 515 BC (the date of the second temple's completion), because the temple mentioned in Joel 2 v 17 must be the second temple given 3 v 1-2. When precisely Malachi and Joel are set during the second temple period is unclear.

thegood**book**
COMPANY

Delighting in the Trinity *Why Father Son and Spirit are such good news!*

Tim Chester

This book aims to help you see how the Trinity is fantastically good news. Because the Trinity means that God is not remote and uninvolved – quite the opposite. God sent His Son and His Spirit into our world to draw us into a wonderful relationship with Himself. This is the God who gives meaning and joy to our lives.

Just Love
Why God must punish sin

Ben Cooper

This book was born out of the author's own struggles with this issue, and he writes with empathy as well as intellectual rigour, answering questions such as: Why can't God just "pass over" wrongdoing? How does "the God who punishes" fit with "the God who is love"? And why is the death of Jesus on a cross the ultimate expression of God's love?

From Creation to New Creation
Making sense of the whole Bible story

Tim Chester

Running through the many gripping and memorable stories the Bible contains is one big story of God's plan for the world He made, and how He brought it about through Jesus Christ. This accessible Bible overview unlocks the storyline of the whole Bible – how God promised and then brought about His plan to save our fallen world.

Order from your friendly neighbourhood Good Book website:
UK & Europe: www.thegoodbook.co.uk • **North America:** www.thegoodbook.com
Australia: www.thegoodbook.com.au • **New Zealand:** www.thegoodbook.co.nz

thegoodbook
COMPANY

At The Good Book Company, we are dedicated to helping individual Christians and local churches grow. We believe that God's growth process *always* starts with hearing clearly what He has said to us through His timeless word—the Bible.

Ever since we started in 1991, we have been striving to produce resources that honour God in the way the Bible is used. We have grown to become an international provider of user-friendly resources to the Christian community, with believers of all backgrounds and denominations using our Bible studies, books, evangelistic resources, DVD-based courses and training courses.

We want to help equip ordinary Christians to live for Christ day by day, and churches to grow in their knowledge of God, their love for one another, and the effectiveness of their outreach. Call us to discuss your needs, or visit your friendly neighbourhood website for more information on the resources and services we provide.

UK & Europe: www.thegoodbook.co.uk
North America: www.thegoodbook.com
Australia: www.thegoodbook.com.au
New Zealand: www.thegoodbook.co.nz

UK & Europe: 0333 123 0880
North America: 866 244 2165
Australia: (02) 6100 4211
New Zealand: (+64) 3 343 1990